# THE ROCK & ROLL TIMES
## GUiDE TO THE MUSiC iNDUSTRY

**howto**books

Please send for a free copy of the latest catalogue:

How To Books
Spring Hill House, Spring Hill Road, Begbroke
Oxford OX5 1RX, United Kingdom
email: info@howtobooks.co.uk
www.howtobooks.co.uk

# THE ROCK & ROLL TIMES

## GUIDE TO THE MUSIC INDUSTRY

THE 10 A & R COMMANDMENTS
ALL BANDS NEED TO KNOW

## WILL BEATTIE

Published by Spring Hill
Spring Hill is an imprint of How To Books Ltd
Spring Hill House, Spring Hill Road
Begbroke, Oxford OX5 1RX
Tel: (01865) 375794. Fax: (01865) 379162
info@howtobooks.co.uk
www.howtobooks.co.uk

British Library Cataloguing in Publication Data
A catalogue record for this book is available from the British
Library

ISBN 978 1 905862 10 8

Cover illustration by Rob Leeks
Produced for How to Books by Deer Park Productions, Tavistock
Typeset by Pantek Arts Ltd, Maidstone, Kent
Printed and bound by Cromwell Press, Trowbridge, Wiltshire

NOTE: The material contained in this book is set out in good
faith for general guidance and no liability can be accepted
for loss or expense incurred as a result of relying in particular
circumstances on statements made in this book. Laws and
regulations are complex and liable to change, and readers should
check the current position with the relevant authorities before
making personal arrangements.

# Contents

Dedicated to Claire.
For making the single biggest difference to my life.
You rocked honey and I miss you...

# Thank You ...

When it comes to writing a book it's never down to the individual to make it all happen. So I would like to thank the following people who helped in the process. Firstly to Nikki and Giles at How To Books for giving me the opportunity. To all the interviewees: The Iron Maiden manager Rod Smallwood. Joel De'ath and Steve Proud at Atlantic Records. Neil Ridley at Warners. Amy Daniels at Lavolta. Mark Palmer at RoadRunner. Peter Chiesa at Stephen Budd management. Myles Keller at MCPS-PRS. Michael Laskow at www.taxi.com. Donal Whelan at www.masteringworld.com Dick Beathum at 360 Mastering Studios. Jon Dunn at Livenation. Nicholas Barnet at Dead or Alive. Mark Gnui at Primary. Andy McIntyre. Natasha Bent at The Agency. Luke Selby at Vital. Sofia Hagberg at End of the Road festival. Paul King and John at www.ukbands.net. Richard Robson at Freak music productions and special thanks goes to Alex Norden at The Agency for everything you have done and for being a mate. Also to Rob Leeks for designing the cover and illustrations, and to Rod and Stella for all the help, advice and friendship over the years.

It's been a long time coming so thanks to my mum and dad for being my mum and dad. To my brothers Alex (and Louise), Andy and Iain (and Louise) for bailing me out over the years. An extra special thank you to Claire and Ed over at www.invey.com for designing and building the original Rock and Roll Times website and for everything else you guys did. It matters as much now as it did then because you got me started. I love you for that (you all need to go to invey.com and buy a CD!). To Barry Rafer Wildash and the flight of the wild geese for keeping me sane this past year and for looking after the house. To Bub Ho Tep for making me laugh. Hey Amigo! To Wing Commander Duncan Woods. Paul Dorritt, Danny Woods, Phil Page, Sheryl Clements, Luis Smith, Kate Grove, Meredith Cork, Joe Ruffalo, Mahesh Shah, Aiden Gilligan, Dom and Alice, and to everyone who I've forgotten don't take it personally, you know I love you.

# Why I wrote this book

The music industry is changing. And you, the musician, the band, the solo artist, are part of that change. Without any of you there is no music industry. You are the single most important aspect of why we all do what we do, but without the bands, the song writers, the ones who can change our lives, there would be a big empty void in all of us. The world has lost valuable songs along the way because some bands didn't make it. The record deal they chased never appeared and so they gave up, and in some strange way, the world lost out.

Being in a band is a life-long process. It's also one of the hardest things in the world to be successful at. And that's the problem. We define far too many things with the word successful. And it's not about that. You are the music makers. If you make music, then you are already successful. You've done your job. Whether you get the chance to play on the world stage is not in your hands and nor should it be used to measure the value of what you have written. The internet has freed bands and with digital technology it has given you the best time in all of human history to create a CD full of music. Once you have done that, the rest is in the hands of fate.

I would hope that the information contained in this book gives you some ideas to think about creating a platform without chasing something that may never come. Yes, that ever elusive recording contract. The digital revolution has truly brought change to every musician and, whilst there will always be a need for record labels, you are no longer limited in the chances that are now open to you. Record labels and the music industry bring you expertise in the many areas you will be involved in – whether it's recording, touring, press and promotion, distribution or management – these are areas that are vital to a band's existence. All of it costs money. And that's the point. We all need money to survive. A band needs a structure around them to exist and develop. But you also need ideas. And this book I hope will leave you feeling like you can go forth and create the life through music you've dreamed about. It's not impossible, but it does take time. Many of you will chase the record deal anyway, and good luck to you, but through implementing the chapters written here, this Rock and Roll Road we are all on may just give you a smoother ride.

I've seen far too many bands struggle and starve. I've seen them literally waste away because the last £30 they had went on rehearsals rather than food. That kind of passion still blows me away. I've seen bands sacrifice personal happiness in the pursuit of musical excellence, leaving me in awe. Because it's that kind of commitment you will all need if you stand any kind of chance of making it in a very overcrowded world.

Each chapter in this book was written to provide you with the ideas, insights and understandings for you to take the world on. It's written with a full perspective to get you thinking for yourself. And should you chase a recording contract and fail, well then you can always come back and learn how to set up a record label, can't you? A band will need the right people around them to guide, help and support them during their career.

And I'm no different. During the writing of this book there were people I needed to help me along. Elliot Chalmers from www.musiclawadvice.co.uk has written all the legal terms and definitions you will find in this book. He also wrote the chapter on music advice. He became a contributing writer after I came across his website and decided to form an alliance as I liked his independent style. Any band seeking further legal advice should stop by Elliot's site.

The next person I enlisted was Rob Leeks who helped me design the book cover and the illustrations for the Ten Commandments. Without Rob's guidance and support, along with artistic talent, those tongue-in-cheek commandments could not have been realised.

The point of the ten commandmants is really to make you think about the most important aspects of what you will do. A&R, songs, how important rehearsals are, touring, press, distribution and creating your CD are the fundamental basics you do need to get right and plan for from the outset. They are also funny because the guy on the front cover is called Unholy Moses and he came down from Mount Rock to deliver the gospel as it was written. You must through all your adventures keep your sense of humour because at times it will be all you have. You can expect to hear a lot more from Unholy Moses on www.therockandroll-times.co.uk as time marches on. Rob can be contacted at robleeks@hotmail.com for any artistic needs you may have.

Donal Whelan from www.masteringworld.com in my opinion wrote the definitive account of what the mastering process is all about. These guys are experts and their love for music is a joy to be around.

Lastly on the recruitment front Mr Andy McIntyre came in at the last minute like a ninja and presented what I think is the best account and definition of the A&R (artist and repertoire) role ever written. It takes you into the mind of the A&R process and gives you the complete understanding of what makes an A&R guy tick. Thanks to all of you.

And so my friends, there can be no more excuses. There has never been a better time for a band to exist. You have the power to take control. You have the platforms to showcase who you are. You have technology that never existed 10, let alone, 30 years ago to record songs at home. I suspect John Lennon is looking down from heaven cursing how lucky you really are. You have an insatiable media searching for new music all the time. You have kids abandoning the computer consoles looking for kick ass bands to go and see. You have everything you could ever need to create a rock and roll life, so get out there and get it done. Email me at info@therockandrolltimes.co.uk and let me know how you are getting on. And yes, I will be interested...

One last thing. There is a band I had in mind during the process of writing this book. Guys, your dedication, passion, hunger, desire and execution in all you do became my inspiration a long time ago to make this book happen. You are the archetype every band should be inspired to be. Your addiction to music was a comfort to me and I salute you forever. Perhaps one day I will see you in Timbuktu!

Now, let's see what all the fuss is about shall we…?

# Approaching the A&R department

i

For those about to Rock – we salute you

Commandment One

When approaching record companies you are essentially approaching the A&R department. They are the ones who decide if you will get signed or not. And it's a hard fact to get into immediately, but most bands in existence will not get that hallowed 'Yes, we love you, and we want to sign you' from the friendly neighbourhood A&R guy. Instead, you will get that pretty bog standard rejection letter on a wet Monday morning with something like...

*We have listened to your songs very carefully, but have decided to pass at this time. Please do bear us in mind for any future projects you may work on...*

Many of you will have been there and I'm sure you can remember what it felt like to read those words. No matter how pragmatic you are it still feels like something has been ripped out of your stomach. Of course, the particular record label was just trying to be nice. But they don't really want to hear from you again.

## MONEY MATTERS

However, it is important to understand a few things. Most A&R personnel do want every CD they hear to be the next big thing. It is disappointing to hear a band that just doesn't cut it. And having been in A&R myself, most bands really don't cut it on a commercial level. There are an estimated three million bands on MySpace worldwide alone and perhaps 1,000 of those have any kind of prospect of getting record company interest, with a possibility of around 500 of them getting signed industry-wide over a period of three years or so. That's not to say the rest of those bands could not have a career on a certain level, it's just that the majority of money the music industry invests in bands does not get recouped.

So the ultimate decision is based on financial considerations. Of course there is also the simple fact that a lot of bands don't have the songs or live performance to generate excitement. Investing in bands is expensive and with today's fast food consumer lifestyles many record companies do not have the time or resources to develop many new artists. The expense is simply too high. With a digital revolution comes a price. Everything has speeded up. That means new bands have to come off the starting block ready to go and if you don't cut it, like a plague of locusts, everyone is onto the next band and so on.

## Time pressure

It's a shameful fact that most bands that do get signed in this day and age are lucky to last three years – let alone three albums. I think that's a statement of the society we live in rather than any facet of the music industry. Bands just don't get the chance to mature or evolve. And with so many bands out there and 100 million pages of newsprint to fill, the magazine world is always shouting about the next great thing. Huge pressure is placed on bands to deliver rather than them being given the time to develop. So-called tastemakers are sought out to pontificate on what's radical or the next best thing. So more money is spent – but if the CD sales don't justify the expenditure the band will be dropped.

## DOING IT FOR YOURSELF

The beauty for the band in that respect means that whilst even ten years ago that would have finished them, in the present age, they can go it alone and do it for themselves. Just look at Marillion and The Blutones. They have built a fan base that never went away. And because they took control of their own destiny and didn't spend vast sums of money they proved they could sustain a career in music after the hatchet from the mighty record company. The purpose of this book is to show you that it's not the be-all-and-end-all when a record label says no. In fact, the purpose of this book is to get you thinking about doing it for yourself. For you to create your own record label and control your own musical destiny. There are many books out there that tell you how to get signed, how you can maximise your potential, from people on the inside who have worked with the world's best selling acts and should know how to make you a success. There are books that promise to get you the personal emails of every A&R guy in the world.

What they don't tell you is the truth. A&R guys don't want bands sending them CDs. They want to find the bands for themselves. In the history of music no band really ever got signed by sending in an unsolicited CD. At least none that can be measured against all those who got rejected.

I'm not promising anything other than an insight, truth, care and of course passion for you to get out there and do it for your self. Like I said earlier, with 3 million bands on MySpace and each one of them emailing or calling A&R guys to check their bands, how realistic is it that they will get a response? Not realistic at all, my friends. Instead, for most of you, time would be better spent focusing on creating your own platform – and then letting the industry come to you. When the music industry comes to you, you will be in a far stronger position to negotiate.

## THE BIG FOUR

There are currently four major record companies in the UK. Known as the big four they are:

- EMI
- Universal
- Warners
- Sony BMG.

Any new band with new songs will generally go to these labels and their subsidiaries, and hope to get interest and then be signed. For most of you this is really a waste of time and money. As you progress through the book you will hopefully understand that with digital technology and the internet there has never been a better time for bands to exist and make a career for themselves. The record labels are running scared because they have to adapt to the technological revolution. They spent the first half of the decade chasing 13-year-old kids downloading their favourite bands' music on mp3, hunting them like the witch finder generals they thought they were, and prosecuting people for illegally finding and sharing music.

## The digital music revolution

Napster was a total revolution in music distribution which the major record companies didn't know how to react to or understand. Firstly, downloading music without paying for it is illegal. And yes, they did have to do something about it. But when you have vast warehouses in China manufacturing hundreds of thousands of CDs with proper covers that get sold down the local market, or as it is now being shanghaied by the company rep selling you three DVDs or CDs for a tenner in the burger bar, you can see that chasing after the kids, who are essentially the lifeblood of the industry, was totally the wrong way to go about things. You can blame the lawyers for that.

Instead it has taken them five further years to understand that the way the new music industry of the future is going means rethinking how the corporate machine can survive. The answer is it cannot. Digital distribution via downloads is the future of getting music to the market place.

The IFPI (**www.ifpi.org**) 2007 digital music report states:

*Record companies' digital music sales are estimated to have nearly doubled in value in 2006, reaching a trade value of approximately US$2 billion (up from $1.1 billion). The split between online and mobile remains fairly equal, but varies substantially across markets estimated to have grown from 5.5 % in 2005 to around 10 % of industry sales for the full year 2006. Single track downloads are estimated to total 795 million in 2006, up 89 % on 2005. Single track downloads and mastertones remain the main digital music formats, but other formats, such as mobile downloads, digital albums, music videos and ringback tones all saw healthy growth.*

*The number of tracks available online doubled to reach over 4 million in the last year. This compares to around 150,000 CD albums available in the biggest 'bricks and mortar' music stores. There are nearly 500 online music services available in over 40 countries worldwide, offering consumers a wide variety of choice and great value.*

This bodes well for unsigned bands as it doesn't take any real expense outside of the initial costs of the recording and having a website to place it for download. If there indeed was any kind of visionary aspect to the thinking of record labels they would have jumped into bed with file sharing networks five years ago and been in a much better position today than they are. Instead, it took Apples iTunes to show the world the future of the music industry. Imagine that, a computer company showing the mighty music industry how to do their job. Every record executive at that point should have been fired.

But then we get to the root of the problem. Too many powerful people had too much vested financial interest in keeping the status quo. It would have meant different business models where the artists would have morally had the deal favouring them. Instead, you can now download music to your phone or iPod but the end result, at the time of writing, is that royalty percentages remain in favour of the labels.

## What's the future?

I am of course skimming the surface here. At present there are many think tanks trying to shape the future of the music industry (**www.musictank.co.uk**) by gathering industry professionals to discuss how the industry needs to change. But I would much rather advise you on how, by using digital technology along with the internet, you can really do it for yourself. Now, let's get on and see what those A&R boys and girls think, do and get up to.

## WHAT DOES A&R STAND FOR?

A&R stands for artist and repertoire. The term relates back to the old music industry days and yes, back then bands and artists were as manufactured as they are now. The term A&R was coined to describe the function of people at record labels who are in charge of finding and developing new talent. Some artists had great vocals and stage presence, but no songs, and some song writers could write hits, but had no star quality. It became the A&R guys' job to search for new talent and place them with hit songwriters.

The function of A&R remains mostly the same today. The A&R process is much more than placing artists with songs. Developing the project includes:

- finding the right producer for the band

- along with a good studio

- and certainly in the early days deciding which songs make it to the album.

## How the A&R guys help

A&R guys are really the band's best friend and many are fantastic at quality control when it comes to hearing which songs are the strongest. They have as much vision as the band and are a great resource for realising potential. The other side of that coin are the bands who become successful and seem to dispense with A&R, mostly to the detriment of their career. There are plenty of heavy hitting bands out there with early success, but with albums that lack quality. Metallica are a case in point. A band can get so huge that nobody stands up and says 'Hang on guys, what the hell are you thinking?' Who can really say St Anger stands up as a quality album. It doesn't, but it's Metallica. Personally, I would have said, 'OK lads, you got that out of your system. Now burn the hard disk and start again'. It's ok to make an album for the sake of it, but to commercially release it was just too painful. I needed a therapist after that album. (Note to Metallica henchmen, stand St Anger next to Master of Puppets and tell me I'm wrong before you come after me with your wolverines.)

The A&R person, certainly in the early days of your career, really is your best friend at your new record company home. It's their job to help you make the best album possible. And their career depends as much on the success of your release as does the future of the band itself.

# HOW DO I GET MY MUSIC TO AN A&R PERSON?

It's been said that the best way to get your music to an A&R person is to get them to come to you. That is easier said than done. If you get through to a record label and the band isn't ready the chances are you will get rejected, so it's best to wait a while until you have developed a fan base before approaching A&R.

Building your profile in your home town and surrounding areas through constant gigs and touring farther afield is the first step in your campaign. If you start to get a good buzz and you are selling copious amounts of your CD then word will get back to A&R and you will find them coming to you. Should you want to call A&R – and if you manage to get through – the process in this digital age is that they will want to check out your MySpace site.

The days where A&R have stacks of unheard CDs piling up on their desks are fast approaching the end. Indeed, Polydor records have established an online submission website for unsigned bands to use. This will be the way the industry will go. And once the particular A&R guy has visited your MySpace site and decides your music is not for him that's it. So, try not to be in too much of a rush to get record company interest. You may not be ready yet and you might just blow a good opportunity. It happens all the time. Bands are too eager and always think they have just recorded the best thing since The Beatles. It's much better to build a profile with lots of journalists raving about you, a good hit rate on the website and a good all-round buzz. And when that happens you won't just get one A&R guy call you up, you will have the whole pack. A&R mostly know each other and word tends to spread like wildfire.

There is nothing more satisfying for a band who have held out, built a good solid fan base and received loads of press, to play a packed-out gig with London's finest A&R in the back fighting over who is going to get to the band first. This is called the industry buzz and when you get this, life is very good indeed.

## Caution

As we are in the section on how to get your music to a label I would urge a word of caution (it doesn't happen so much these days but it is worth commenting on). **Any company you come across that offers to get your music to an A&R guy on a compilation CD for a charge should always be avoided.** To me this is just a rip off, a scam, and to justify the charges as admin is totally bogus. There are some companies who do provide this service for free, for example **www.matchboxrecordings.co.uk** who do get their compilations to A&R guys. They are worth a look at, but be aware that you will be on a CD with 20 other bands. It's a good way for A&R to check out bands in one swoop, but it does not increase your chances of any kind of deal. Any company that otherwise charges you to be included in some kind of music industry CD needs to be avoided, and never sign a contract without getting legal advice. So, in short, stay away from them.

## WHAT MAKES AN A&R PERSON WANT TO SIGN YOU?

Essentially this boils down to the only thing that can get you signed. Killer hit songs that can change lives. And that's a pretty big order to fill. And as most bands never get a chance to really speak with industry professionals it's becoming *de rigueur* for bands to do their own artist development. That means you have to be very professional very quickly. If you are proving time and again, via direct selling of CDs from the website or gigs along with downloads, then you have shown to the music industry that the public want what you have. And if people can't get in the door at gigs then this makes A&R very excited. There is a formula (see below) which you can use, like a checklist, and it may be interesting to see how closely you identify with it. I got the basic idea from an article I came across at **www.taxi.com**, which I adapted. I think it gives you a good breakdown of what A&R look for. Either way it's not unique and it does seem obvious when you read it, but I still get amazed at how many CDs I get through the post with more than half of these ingredients missing.

## The A&R formula

### Songs

This is the single most essential ingredient. Think of your favourite band and remember how you felt when you first heard their music. How did it make you feel? Was your life different from that day on? Did the hairs on the back of your neck stand up? Did your stomach do flips, etc. And if the kids don't want to play air guitar to even one of your songs then it's time to get back to the drawing board. You get what I'm saying. Songs are life changing. And already this is the level you are up against. There has to be a vibe running through a song that tells the listener they cannot live a day or an hour without hearing your music. You have to touch them on an emotional level. Songs should either make you want to feel like going nuts, or cry, feel happy, sad, or at least jump up and down. You become a milestone in a person's life. The day they really started to become who they are as people is the day you became the soundtrack to their existence. And how do you do this?

### Passion

Passion is belief in what you are writing and playing. Lyrics need to have meaning and music needs to have soul. Music is an art form dealing purely in inner emotion. It's an intangible feeling that can take you to a higher plane of existence. If you don't have the belief then you cannot transfer the emotional content to a song. This is what gives the connection to the audience. Passion is the lifeblood that fuels the songs you are writing. If you are not in touch with your self emotionally then you will not be able to touch anybody else. This is what makes an artist an artist.

### Live show

The live show is the biggest entity a band needs to be aware of. You are putting on a show to entertain people. A great live performance will win fans for life and likewise a poor live performance will turn people off. This is where you communicate who you are as a band. Some bands who have great songs do not always play great shows. And then there are bands with average songs but seem to be on fire live. A good live show is essential in getting record company interest and even more important in winning fans. Some bands seem to lack emotion when playing live. I've seen bands play the local venue to three people with a killer live performance. It shouldn't matter to a band if they play to 20 people or 2,000, the attitude has to be there. Your live performance defines who you are. The total belief a band has in themselves should be evident from the very first note to the last. Also, if you blow an audience away with a great live show the first thing they do when you leave the stage is go and buy your CD and t-shirt. And ultimately this is how you will make your living.

## Charisma

This is something that cannot be controlled or planned for. It's that mystery ingredient called the X factor. Charisma shines like a star and makes ego-centric people create cults. The larger-than-life character in any band is almost always the singer. Star quality can make up for a lack of talent, but what it lacks in talent it makes up for in iconology. All great bands have had someone who ordinary people want to be like. KISS had four members in makeup and created space age superheroes that have endured over 30 years. Metallica have James Hetfield. Iggy Pop has Iggy Pop and likewise David Bowie has David Bowie. No one can deny that the two biggest members in Oasis are Noel and Liam. There is something about these characters that has an element of danger and excitement. If you try to act it you will be denounced as a fake in very short order. So, you either have it or you don't. And if you don't, you need to get someone in the band who has. It will make the difference between cool and generic. Charisma makes people want to be you. It still makes me laugh when I see Slipknot at a gig and the kids are all in jumpsuits. Which leads us on nicely to…

## Marketability

Image. Who really would have said that nine guys in jumpsuits and masks would take the world by storm before Slipknot hit the world stage? The image for this band worked perfectly. It gave them the edge during a time when music was once again redefining itself. Nine guys on stage with baseball bats beating up drums created a spectacle that defined what a live performance is all about. And in doing so created a fantastic marketing ploy the press could not get enough of. Slipknot are a good example of marketability. You see what the band is and know who will buy the CDs. In this case, the kids. The age group of 13–24-year-old males is how the marketing department would have seen it. That would be the core group and obviously anyone into heavy music. The example is a simple one but effective. Heavy music across the world is huge. And Slipknot had the edge straight away. We shall stay with Slipknot for the next ingredient…

## Group focus

This is all about direction and where the band is going. Each member of Slipknot has a role to play. Whether it's research, art, politics, etc, the whole band moves and thinks as one. It's them against the world. And you can bet that anyone aligned to the band from the manager to the roadies has the same thought process. Slipknot had the plan and all they needed from the record company was the finance to realise that. Your band has to have that same direction. And with digital technology band roles outside of playing can be website development, merchandise development, stage show development, etc, etc. It's the game plan the band will hatch onto the world and it is very effective. As the saying goes, fail to plan, plan to fail.

## Hunger

Hunger to get to the top through sheer force of will can either make or break bands. How hungry are you? How easy have you had it so far? And what are you not prepared to do to hit the big time? Whilst most of your friends have jobs, mortgages, girlfriends, nice shoes and the latest fashionable clothes and money in the bank, the average band will be a starved, skint, rag wearing, baked bean eating machine running up and down the motorways of the UK at 3 in the morning existing on hamburgers and beer. It's a hard road ahead and your sheer determination and hunger may falter from time to time, but can never run out. When it does, it's the end of the journey and you get to rejoin the human race. I've seen bands live in vans with gas cookers, surviving on eggs and pot noodles. But this is how it is. If you are too comfortable with all the mod cons, play stations, DVDs and in the pub every night then you don't have that hunger to succeed. You have to earn the right to get signed. And this means being driven. To the point of obsession.

## Business sense

This area concerns your management more than the band. Along with the lawyer and accountant, the band should be talked through all business proposals and deals. The band should make sure they have a team in place they trust so the band can get on with the job in hand, writing music and playing live. Ultimately the band is a business that creates a product. It's important from the start that you understand this. At some point the band will have to sit down and discuss the business life of the band.

## Trap doors

Considering the business you are in, i.e., rock and roll, this area will always be under scrutiny. Band members with problems with either alcohol or drugs will become a liability. If you have a big, expensive world tour in the wings and the singer is strung out to the point where they can't perform, this will lead to huge problems. Any problems with money, personal issues, members with attitudes, etc, need to be fixed as soon as they arise. Problems out on the road don't get better so they should be sorted before the band commit to long-term goals. Otherwise it can lead to break ups. Record labels are very sensitive to their artists self destructing and, whilst most will tolerate a certain amount of eccentricity, alarm bells will ring if the band soon gets out of control.

## A&R INSTINCT

The A&R guy's instinct is what they need to sell you to the record label. They will go into the big A&R meeting and declare their undying love for everything the band stands for. Ultimately it's always a risk signing bands. And with estimates of up to 1 million pounds to market and promote bands many do put their jobs on the line. So, instinct plays a big role. They may be the only guy at the label who really believes in the band from the start. It's worth noting that when A&R departments underperform and new management is brought in, the entire A&R team are dispensed with. So, have an understanding of what A&R go through to get bands signed. The careers of bands and A&R often go hand in hand.

### The process of looking at a band with a view to signing them

A&R will have computed these ingredients through their radar in a nano second. These guys are experts. When you spend so much time listening to bands and seeing them live, you do become very good at knowing who has IT and who does not. And this takes us on to the next bit. Unless you enter the A&R guy's radar they will not care about you. They do not have the time in the day to return your call, have a conversation or be your friend. And don't take any of it personally. The average A&R day is spent in meetings, looking after the bands they already have signed, more meetings, sorting mixes for the new record, talking to producers, dealing with managers, avoiding record label politics, some more meetings, catching a rehearsal or two and finally, after all that, maybe getting the chance to hear some new demos, grabbing a bite to eat before heading out to a gig. That happens every day so don't get the huff if they don't call you back and never ever expect a response or take offence if they can't. If they get what you are doing they will call you. Remember, there are 3 million bands on MySpace, they are far too busy getting through each one.

### Demos and digital

Every A&R guy really does want to find the one band that can make the difference. But unless they love you, you will never get that call. And it's worth adding here that in March 2007 Sony/BMG labels announced two of its record labels are to stop accepting unsolicited physical demos. Instead it was setting up websites to accept digital recordings only. Essentially this is really to stop any band from sending in material in the hope of being discovered, leading the music industry to finally find a way to prevent their offices becoming more overcrowded with music nobody has the time to hear. This will release man power time to listen to acts digitally, save costs in sending CDs back and put a stop to receiving phone calls from bands and managers. They will now control their digital domains and not have to face hopeful acts with bad news. It will save bands money, etc, but you need to understand that **this will be the way the entire record label pack will do business from this point on.**

This leads me on to the next point. And one that goes against what most of the other books on the music industry or even websites will tell you. **No band ever got signed by sending in an unsolicited demo to a record label.** And mostly, it's a complete waste of time and expense. You don't need to write nice demo submission letters, you don't need to tell the A&R guy how passionate you are, and you don't need to do any of the crap you read about from the media on how to approach the record industry. Why? Because it simply does not work. You are better off, if you really need to learn the hard way, to email the company for them to check out your website. You will get a quicker response. It's always better for a band to play live and build a following, raising its profile and letting the A&R come to you. A&R will seek out tips from studios, journalists, DJs, managers, agents and promoters to name just a few sources.

### Seeing you live

The next stage after the A&R guy has heard you is to pop along to see you live. If they are blown away by the gig and they love the music then the ante is upped very quickly. A&R will know you are the real deal and you will not be a secret for long. They will see their A&R manager very quickly and get them down to have a look at you. If at this stage all goes well your manager will be invited in for a formal chat. Don't be surprised if you are being courted by a few A&R guys at this stage. This generally tends to get bands feeling very loved, wanted and special indeed. Some bands will let their egos get in the way and having a pack of A&R chase after you can seriously affect a band's judgment.

## THE RECORD DEAL

Getting a record deal is when the real hard work starts and the clock is ticking. I would always advise that the most money offered is not always the best deal given. I would go to the label with the A&R guy who understands what the band stands for and can therefore deliver what the band needs. The ins and out of any record deal are very specific to the band signing.

We can, however, state generally what a record deal means. The band would most likely be courted by the A&R department, and shown a good time and how great the record company is. The manager's job is to make ready the band's lawyer and discuss with the A&R guy what he has in mind. An offer will be tendered and that's when your management and lawyer sit you down to explain exactly what's on offer.

*When The Darkness sold out the Astoria, Mushroom Records in the shape of A&R man Joel De'ath (now Atlantic Records) had been on the case from day one. However, Mushroom were not in a position to sign the band until they were taken over by Warners. Atlantic Records was resurrected as a label and made the band an offer. Sony at this point offered the band a lot more money, but with limits. The Darkness opted to sign with Atlantic because they were able to keep the team that had grown with them. Must Destroy Records, who had signed The Darkness initially, were then absorbed into the Warner group and the band went on to please and confuse the public in equal measure. The band and their management made a good business move on their part and launched Atlantic Records in a blaze of glory.*

## What is a record deal?

A record deal, also known as a recording contract, is a legally binding document between an artist and a production or record company. Usually prepared by the record company's solicitors, it is then negotiated between them and the artist's management and lawyer.

The main purpose of a deal is to give the record company rights to use or sell recordings of the artist's performances – to exploit the recordings. A recording of a song and the song itself are handled separately and thus attract separate rights.

The history of the recording contract shows that many stars of yesteryear whose songs are still covered by major artists today, paid on the basis of their original contracts, receive pennies rather than pounds in royalties. In addition, artists may not have been paid on the actual number of records sold, instead royalties were sometimes calculated on only 90 per cent of sales! This dates back to the age of 78 vinyl records when an average 10 per cent would break in transit. There are countless stories to be found in numerous rock stars' autobiographies documenting much exploitation verging on slavery, usually resulting in the artists losing out badly financially.

- Although times have changed contracts are still inevitably biased in favour of the record companies, who control the master recordings and charge or recoup the full amount of production costs to the artist's 'possible' royalty account, leaving them with an outstanding debt unless the recordings are hugely successful.

- The record label may pay for the manufacturing costs of CDs, audio cassettes, etc, but beware! A 'packaging deduction' is taken from the artist's royalty, these expenses cover the cost of CD/cassette covers, artwork, etc, are hugely overcharged and rarely bear any relation to the actual cost... To repeat, anything that is paid for by the record company on behalf of the artist is recoupable from their royalties, so in effect they act like a bank who *loans* you money to record your works. The artist has to repay all expenditure.

- Even after the costs have been recouped the company still owns the royalties to the album. If the sales are low, then all possible future royalties from later albums or projects are taken to pay off the artist's debt! Known as cross-collateral, this is something that can be avoided if you have your contract properly analysed by a lawyer who is willing to insist on inserting clauses that redress the balance of the contract.

So, how does the music industry qualify such a practice? Artists are often offered long, unrealistic contracts for huge advances. The label view is that they spend large sums developing and signing artists knowing there is a chance they may never sell commercial quantities of songs. They have to continue to market and promote their current successful artists and re-invest in new talent.

Another sting in the tail is the practice of shelving or ditching an act/band if the A&R person leaves the company or fails to develop or promote the artist or their recordings. This has left many talented musicians out of pocket with no control of their recordings, tied into a contract with a company which no longer has an interest in their material, but retains all the copyright royalties until the artist's debt is repaid.

The recording contract has evolved over the years, but essentially the model still rests on the full assignment of rights to the label. I have seen some signs of change with deals involving a part assignment, but this is very rare as the industry struggles to adapt to differing attitudes.

## Types of deals

### Production company deals

These only provide creation and ownership of recordings, relying on licence arrangements with real record companies to release, market and distribute recordings. There are several drawbacks to this type of agreement:

1. Production companies owned and run by managers take ownership rights to their artists' recordings, enabling the manager to receive a profit on his licence deals plus the management commission, **although this should be negotiated before signing**.

2. A full hourly or daily rate for studio time may be added to the artist's debt to be recouped against royalties. It is obviously in their interest to encourage the artist to use as much studio time as possible!

3. The copyright in your master recordings may still be owned by the company after the term of contract and if they go bust all royalty payments will be used by the creditors to pay their outstanding debts. **Make sure you have termination and reversion of rights clauses in this eventuality**.

4. Recoupment can be complicated. **This is where an accountant can help you**.

5. An overall licence containing several artists signed to the production company may be cross-collateralised (see earlier), using the most successful artist's royalties to cover the losses of failed acts.

## *Licence deals*

This is where the artist has funded the cost of recording, retains all rights including copyright and has all rights to their work returned to them on expiry of contract. This still grants the company the rights to manufacture, distribute and sell agreed recordings, but the artist/songwriter/band retains some control over artwork, distribution and exploitation, receives an improved royalty rate and pays less packaging deductions.

## *Profit split deals*

Small independent labels with limited funding will negotiate a profit split where they agree to deduct all expenditure from income and then split the profits at an agreed percentage with the artist. The payments received can vary considerably depending on the success or failure of the albums sales. **This is the most likely first time deal for a band and can teach you how to spot costs and see how your income is affected by them.**

# Main terms of a record deal

## *Number of recordings*

The deal will state the amount of recordings an artist/band has to deliver (minimum commitment is usually one album) to the record company during a specified period of time (term). **Avoid long contracts, ten-album deals, etc, unless the record company contracts to significantly develop the artist's career.**

It should be noted that a record company does not guarantee to release the artist's recordings at all, release depends on commercial acceptance by the company. Get a good lawyer to change this to 'technically acceptable', which marginally lessens the record company's leeway. If accepted the company will be obliged to agree a 'release commitment', which is a guarantee to release the album or singles.

Options should be inserted if not already there. It splits up the term length and the rights to more recordings from the artist.

For instance, a five-album deal would actually be a one- or two-album deal with options for the record company to renew the contract at the end of each period. These are referred to as the 'Initial Period' followed by the 'First Option Period', etc.

### Exploitation, rights and territories including cable and satellite transmissions

To ensure the record company has exclusive rights on all recordings an artist agrees not to make recordings and/or videos for anyone else, grants permission for the company to hold the copyrights on all recordings, manufacture, distribute and sell their recordings in specific countries (Territories) for an agreed period which will include 're-recording restrictions' preventing the artist from re-recording tracks previously released. Artists may have performances recorded, and guest appearances on other artists' records are usually permitted, but require consent, a written credit on the album cover and sometimes payment to the artist's record company. There will also be a clause granting the record company the right *not* to any of the above if it so chooses!

### Artist royalty percentages, basis of calculations and payment periods

Unknown artists will have less negotiating power than established acts who can command higher royalty percentages and advances. Once the first album is released and a return is shown, the next contract period or option renewal should allow the artist's solicitor to renegotiate a slightly better percentage or sliding scale with each successful release.

### Advances against royalties and instalment periods

Advances are payments made against future royalties. Payments in each contract period are paid in instalments from the date of signing and on delivery of the 'Minimum Commitment'. The payment terms are usually negotiable with the artist, who receives either lump sums or monthly instalments.

### Recoupable costs payable before the artist receives royalty payments

Seemingly huge advances are soon whittled down when you realise that from the initial advance your manager will take 20% (dependent on the terms of your management deal) and the monies paid will have to support you totally, including recording costs, income tax and national insurance deductions, living costs, etc, for one to two years. All advances and recoupable costs, including deductions for packaging, production, art work, are added together for the period during which the artist is signed and all income/royalties are used to repay these costs. In addition, the artist's royalties are usually calculated on the discount or trade price, not the full retail price of their recordings, and in the case of special products such as TV-advertised albums, are only paid at 1/2 or 2/3 of the contractual rate even after all the other deductions!

It is quite common for an artist to earn no money from royalties and end up in debt to the company. Generating other forms of income via touring or publishing and merchandising deals is a necessity!

### Other terms

Other terms including publishing, group provisions, music video rights, equipment, tour support, producers, accounting, promotional duties, termination, creative and cost control are all minefields of legalese. They are written in favour of the record company, with miscellaneous indemnity provisions to prevent the artist suing the company in the event that not enough effort was made to promote, distribute, sell more records and giving the company the right *not* to deliver any of the above if it so chooses!

> *Never* verbally agree or sign any form of agreement without seeking advice from a qualified solicitor specialising in the music industry. Believe it or not, verbal agreements *are* legally binding!

*Never* verbally agree or sign any form of agreement without seeking advice from a qualified solicitor specialising in the music industry. Believe it or not verbal agreements *are* legally binding!

## BREAKING INTO A&R

Many of you will be interested in becoming A&R guys yourselves. It's a good life, full of fun, but lots of hard work and very difficult to break into. A&R jobs are almost never advertised and the way most break into it is by getting to know someone at a label who can recommend you when a vacancy comes up. Most labels have graduate schemes, and it's worth looking at the human resource sections at all the majors and applying when you leave university. This will give you a good understanding of how labels work and a foot in the door.

Firstly though, do not go expecting that it will be a walk in the park. You will have to know your stuff before even thinking about applying. The best way to do this if you are at university is to get involved in the ents department and start helping with booking bands. The best way to enter A&R is about to be disclosed, and will apply if you are at uni or just trying to break into the music industry. It worked for me and it can for you. Bear in mind that there are very few vacancies for A&R so you will have to rely on good old-fashioned hard work and a little bit of luck. But you do need to be in the arena to stand a good chance and obviously move to London if you are serious about a gig at a record label.

### Stage one of doing your homework

Before approaching a record label about A&R and work experience there will be a mass of competition vying for the same job. The one person to get the coveted chance will be the one who does their homework. You should go in there knowing the unsigned scene around the UK like you are an expert and make the record label want to invest in you. It doesn't matter which town you are from in the UK as most will have a music scene. It goes without saying that if you are in a small village in the Shetlands, whilst you can rely on the internet, you do need to get yourself to a city to experience live music and generate contacts. You will have to submerge yourself in the unsigned band culture and get to know almost every single band out there. You will be out three or five fives times a week at your local music venue until you get to know which bands exist in your home town music scene. This is your first stage.

## Stage two of doing your homework

Get to know every single town's music scene. This is how you do it. In almost every town there will be a music venue. Your job is to get onto the gig listing of every venue and start getting to know the music scene of every town. Each month music venues mail out gig listings for the bands playing the venue. Study which bands are unsigned by checking out their websites and getting hold of their CDs. See every band that comes to your town and, if you can, go and visit other towns to see as many others as possible. If you are part of your uni ents team then start to get involved in bringing bands to your town.

You have now started your A&R mission. This will take a few months of hard work, getting to know on a high level the state of play of the UK unsigned music industry. Get yourself onto websites that deal with unsigned bands. Get as much info on each band as you can and start the sifting process of which bands you think will get deals or have created a buzz. If you get involved in promoting new bands then you will start to make contacts from all over. Do not be afraid to say you are a freelance A&R scout as this will build your confidence in what you are doing. I would start making compilation CDs and then start to get to know A&R personnel at record labels. You should aim to have a good solid working knowledge of 200 acts at any one time and, considering in London alone there are around 5,000 bands playing each month, this gives you an idea of what you are up against UK-wide.

When you start getting to know A&R guys, this is easier in London than elsewhere, ask if it's ok to start sending in your compilations. This needs to be kept up to at least one compilation a month so you stick in their mind. At some point an opportunity will come up where you get the chance to get some work experience at a label and this will be your major chance. Expect to give your life over to this, to be out almost every night during the week, with lots of time researching over the internet and listening to new music. This is the foundation you will need if you want to give yourself the best chance of breaking into the music industry.

Oh, and it will all be done for free. It will be a long time before you get paid, so do not go thinking you will be walking into a paid position anytime soon. A lot of labels do use regional A&R scouts, and if you get to that point you may get expenses paid and certainly get into gigs for free.

## Your complilation

Each compilation should have a song or two from the bands you have listed along with a brief bio of who they are and where they come from. You should also mention why the band are in your hot list. This will come easier the more you do it, but you must remain professional. Placing friends' bands on there will backfire if they do not stand up to scratch. You will make mistakes and you will have setbacks but keep going. If you don't get the response you expected from labels just keep at it. Record labels are looking for dedicated, passionate and hungry people to invest in.

So, the competition is fierce, don't be meek and make sure you build your knowledge and make it extensive. If there are styles of music you are not clued up on make it a daily study to get to know that style better. Don't just stick to your favourite style and do not go looking to sign copycats of your favourite bands. If the bands you submit get rejected do not take it personally and understand why they have been rejected. Ask questions, ask what kind of bands the label is looking for. You are like a fisherman, throw out your nets and await the catch. Sift, then bring the catch home. Remember, there are 3 million bands on MySpace and more forming each week. You have a lot of fun ahead of you, so enjoy.

So, firstly, get to know your home town music scene thoroughly. Then branch out to the rest of the UK one town at a time. Some towns have more than one venue so get onto the gig list of every venue. Get to London as much as you can and get to know the Camden scene. This will help you gain the experience you need and will open up doors to the industry. You have to prove yourself and the only way to do that is to jump in. Read all the magazines and websites with job listings, as sometimes A&R scouts are called for and this could be a good opening for you. You cannot be told how to do everything, but what I've mentioned so far is a good solid way to break into the music industry. The rest will be down to how hungry you are, how much music industry sense you have and trusting your instincts. If from the start you believe you are an A&R scout, then through doing the work, you are waiting for an opportunity to deliver the goods. Belief will make it real.

## INSIGHTS FROM A&R PEOPLE

To finish off this section I spoke to a couple of current A&R people to get an added insight.

### Steve Proud: Atlantic Records

*My role at Atlantic is in the capacity of A&R scout. The road to A&R for me started back at uni. I went through playing in bands but realised I didn't have the knack for writing songs. I knew I wanted to be involved in the music industry so I thought it best to focus on a creative level linked to either PR or actually in A&R. So I chose a university in a town where I knew there was a very active music scene. I just wanted to get to as many gigs as possible and that was really my only requirement.*

*I have to say I thought the industry was such a hard place to break into I didn't have a plan, like X,Y or Z to follow which would lead me into a record label. I just wanted to see loads of bands. I went to Bristol University and just submerged myself in music. From there I got involved in student media and ended up writing reviews for the student paper. I was out at gigs four times a week and through that got to know loads of people and expand my awareness of bands. From reviews I went onto writing features and interviewing bands, which was a great way to get into shows for free and meet my favourite artists. This gave me insights into what makes bands tick and how they go about doing things, which developed my strength as a writer.*

*The next stage took me into student radio, where I had two shows a week. I ended up as head of music and I found through doing it that I was getting new music six weeks before it was released to the public. I got involved in club nights, getting new music played and helping with the ents team in being involved with the bands that came to play. I'd help with the load in, meet the band and make sure they were happy, sort the rider out and whatever else that needed to be done.*

*Through all of this I had developed relationships with certain labels who I sent my chart and playlists to and decided in my final year to ask if there were any internships coming up. I applied for the graduate trainee scheme at Warners, along with 1,500 other people, and went through interviews which led me to getting the gig as press assistant six months later. I then found myself going from two to three shows a week to two to three shows each night!*

▶

*During this time I had come across three bands I thought were particularly cool, Pure Reason Revolution, Snowfield and Editors. I'd given Editors their first gig out of Birmingham when I was at Bristol and had watched them develop. Word was spreading around the industry about the band just after I gave the CD to the A&R department, who called me in and asked if I wanted to join them. I'd scouted three bands that had created an industry buzz. I was given the chance to develop in A&R further.*

*It was at this point that I completely abandoned the rest of my life and became even further entrenched in music. I lived and breathed music and totally committed myself to finding quality new acts to sign.*

*As for my day-to-day life, we have an open demo policy here. Any demo that finds itself to us will get listened to. Even if it's just a 30 second blast one of us will listen to it. I get around five to 15 CDs a day and I will listen to all of them. But I have to add I am aware that we are one of the few labels that continue to accept unsolicited submissions. Then there's online research. I'll look at the listings and find out who's playing where and get my gig diary sorted. I will then speak to managers, agents, promoters, press, lawyers and of course bands. The other side is at rehearsals, gigs, being in the studio during recording sessions, listening to mixes and talking to producers.*

*What I look for in a band is songs. The songs have to be great or, if its early days, then the showing of potential has to shine through. Demo-wise, the first thing I look for is whether the singer can sing. I'm not looking for technical vocals, but more of a charisma to their voice. We still get far too many demos with out of tune vocals and they just go straight to the bin. Band-wise, are they doing anything slightly different to what's already current? Mediocrity seems to be becoming more and more accepted by younger bands who just want to emulate their favourite artists. This is a guarantee their demo would get rejected.*

*I'm always looking for something unique and special. However, it's hard to define that. Which makes it worthwhile when you do find something that is different. The one question I ask is if I would buy an act's CD in HMV over the other 50 releases that week. And that's the same for anyone into music. What is it that makes you want to buy a band's CD? It comes down to the songs every time. And that is essentially great vocals, great melodies and great tunes. If I'm going to take a project on I'm going to be working it every hour of every day of every week. I've got to have the belief that the people out there are going to find it as life affirming as I did when I first listened to it. If you have a kid working in a shop selling jeans on a Saturday and they have £15 to spare, what's going to make them buy one CD over another one? It's that kind of quality I'm looking for that would make that kid buy a CD.*

*It's the same with a live performance. A good show should be captivating. It has to draw you in. The image of the band at that point doesn't really matter as that can change with some time or money, but if you come away from a show thinking 'wow', and that's after knowing what they sound like because you've checked their website out, I would definitely have a deeper look.*

*It's always encouraging to see bands self-release 500 singles and selling them out or booking a number of gigs packing the venues. For most bands that is a great foundation. This is where a major label would start to have a look as activity has started to be generated. This is always a better way for a band to go than just sending out CDs in the hope of getting a record deal. It may not always be possible for a major label to get involved until that point, but it's showing from the band's perspective that what they are doing is working. And that itself is the building block of success.*

## Joel De'ath: Atlantic Records

*I'm the A&R manager here at Atlantic. How I got involved in A&R was that I simply went to loads and loads of gigs. Every half-decent band I thought I should see, I went and saw. I listened to every type of music, not just my personal interests, but everything. This gave me depth to understanding different styles of music. I then jumped at the chance to do a two-week work experience placement at Music For Nations which led to me staying there for nine months. I'm a big metal fan so I knew a lot about the bands they had signed, Cradle of Filth especially at that time. I then went to V2 and onwards to Mushroom Records which is quite a funny story. At the time of the work experience, which you don't get paid for, I was working in a bakery. I had a friend there who wanted to break into the music industry and had sent out loads of CVs which led to him being offered a gig at Abbey Road studios. He had also been offered a two-week placement at Mushroom and asked me if I wanted to go instead.*

▶

*That placement led me to a full-time position. Warners then took over Mushroom some years later, leading to Atlantic Records being resurrected. I was then able to repay that friend by making him the A&R coordinator here five years later. And in a strange way that's how a lot of A&R end up getting gigs. You just have to be out there every night seeing bands, getting to know people, following up calls and then seeing more bands.*

*The real break for me was during the transition process from Mushroom to Warners. I remember picking up a copy of* The Fly *magazine and reading a live review of this band called The Darkness. I then checked out the single, and I went and saw the band at The Monarch around February 2002 which just blew me away. I just thought they were genius and I went back to the label and banged on about it. The momentum for that band had started to build up, but I had kept up a working relationship with the band manager Sue Whitehouse, which helps as there is a trust level being built. When it came time for the band to sign to a deal they chose Atlantic: I will never forget that Justin (Darkness singer) took my boss aside and said the band wouldn't sign unless I was taken over to the new label. Which I always thought was a really nice thing. And then from there things became proper.*

*What I look for in bands now has slightly changed. It's not always just about great songs. I think bands I now work with have an absolute vision and dedication to their art. I'm seeing a pattern emerge where the band's sole reason for being on the planet is to create an audio/visual experience. It's their purpose and that kind of dedication chokes you up. I wish I had that kind of vision because I admire that so much. And now I'm able to look at artists who perhaps haven't got those great songs yet but they have that hunger. They are gigging, writing constantly, playing amazing live shows and busting their guts to create something special. Some of these bands are meeting the kids after their shows, heading back to the fan's house doing another gig, playing car parks, front rooms, outside in the garden, giving away free stuff and I just love that kind of passion. These are the kinds of bands that are changing how we as A&R guys do our job.*

*Personally I will listen to CDs and check out websites. And I have to say that if the music is good it will get signed. And what I love about Myspace is that it's turning kids into A&R people. So they are not being told anymore by the NME what they should or shouldn't like. The NME isn't music it's print, you can't hear print. Whereas on a website there is nowhere to hide. You hear the music and you know if you like it or not straightaway. So the power of the music press has diminished as the kids discover brand new music for themselves. And I think this leads to where bands are heading. You will see more bands releasing more product, more releases with less songs than you would have on a traditional CD, but released on a digital EP. This will lead to shorter tours in support of that release, but the frequency of those releases will be every nine months rather than every 18 months.*

*There will always be a need for A&R guys because there will always be a need for experienced people to find the really good stuff. The quality control will reach a higher level as there will more much more music to sift through. And the reason why bands need A&R boils down to this. There are two types of people that surround any band. In the blue corner you have A&R, managers, lawyers, accountants, etc, who look after the band and develop them. In the red corner you have press, DJs, fans and hangers on, in other words people who adore them.*

*So musicians tend to digress to almost being like a toddler, where they can do anything and people go 'hey aren't you great' and if they slip over these people will catch them. I always think of A&R and to a certain extent some good managers as that grip back to reality where we go 'that ain't good enough'. Sometimes bands go for months if not years without hearing those words. And of course they get offended and cry and throw their toys out of the pram. But an A&R's job is to state the facts and not pander to egos. If something isn't good enough then it's my job to say try harder. I'm not there to be a 'yes' man. Bands have enough 'yes' men surrounding them. My job is to get the best creative output a band can manage during the course of their career. And I'm sure there are many bands who wished they had a lot more people caring about them saying no when it mattered, than being part of some celebrity machine as their careers headed towards the toilet.*

## Neil Ridley: Warners

*Being involved in A&R is really about luck, who you know and being in the right place at the right time. About six years ago I was working for a charity called Youth Music and through that I had made quite a few contacts with managers, labels, rehearsal and recording studios. And this led to me meeting the head of A&R at BMG Records who took me on as a freelance scout. I then spent the next six months running around London to every gig I could get to, getting hold of demos, speaking to managers and studios and building a heavy network of bands that I had seen. This was still whilst I had a day job so it was a pretty intensive six months getting stuck in with no life. I would do a full day at the office then head out to gigs and get home around midnight. But after six months I was taken on as a full-time A&R scout for BMG, so all that hard work paid off, plus I was bringing in some really good bands.*

*I was thrust straight into working with bands like Spiritualised and Natalie Imbruglia, who probably didn't need an A&R guy, but the process taught me how to relate to the artists and that it was important to be diplomatic in dealing with people.*

*From BMG I moved to Warners where I signed The Subways and also brought in Transgression Records who we now work very closely with. I have to say to anyone wanting to break into A&R that it's simply about perseverance and dedication. It's not the glamorous world as portrayed by the media. Well, certainly not when you are being sent to Rotherham on a wet Monday night to see if a band is good or bad. And you are always looking for that band that excites you. When it comes to bands labels like to see a certain amount of development from the band. That's not to say that a band in its early stages wouldn't be taken on, it's just that most bands need to spend some time just being a band before they seek out a record deal. And the only the way any band can do that is to simply keep writing songs and playing live...*

## Amy Daniels: Lavolta Records

*After I finished my degree in Manchester I decided I wanted to work in music so I moved to London. Through a friend I was able to get a one day a week work experience gig over at Lizard King which for me was brilliant. I instantly picked up on what the record label was, and how it was run and what was needed from me. Before that I hadn't had any record label experience at all so I just absorbed as much as I could. I was interested, inquisitive and asked loads of questions. After a few weeks of settling in I got the chance for it to become full time. During this time I just hit the streets and got to know all the promoters, the venues, managers, bands, agents and anyone connected to the music industry. I had already done that in Manchester where I knew everyone, but now it was a case of getting to know everyone again, not just in London but throughout the UK.*

*Part of this process was making compilation CDs of all the good bands I had seen. I'd make notes on each band, who they were, who their manager was, where they were from, where I had seen them, and everything else that was relevant to that band. My boss was monitoring this at the time and asked if I wanted to be part of A&R full time as label people can either be part of the marketing machine or actually in the trenches doing A&R watching bands. I definitely wanted to be in A&R full time finding bands. Lavolta was then set up and I was into the A&R department where I was involved in not just A&R but marketing, research and whatever else was needed of me. It's given me grounding in how a label works from different areas and seeing how it all ties in.*

*Later I became involved in scouting full time for Lavolta as my boss said it's not really something I should continue doing half and half in. If you are doing odd jobs here and there the scouting aspect can get sidetracked. You need to be on it full time when it comes to A&R as things can move that quickly finding bands. I then spent the next month on the road going to Bristol, Brighton, Cardiff, Leeds and Sheffield amongst other cities. I essentially had to make friend with promoters, managers, venues, studios and get to know everyone. I basically had to get to know the UK like I had known Manchester.*

*When it comes to looking at bands they have to have songs that stick in my head. They need to have melodies where you want to hear that song again a day or so later. I also want to see a dynamic within the band. How they look, how they come across, are they all for one. With some bands you see*

▶

*there may be a member who looks like they don't fit or want to be there, or even one member where it's all about them, the me me me syndrome. So, I want to see that gang mentality shine through. And you want to see that the band is together. You can tell if a band is rehearsed, they have a look about them. So any kind of advice I would give to a band is firstly, it's all about the songs. It's better to write three killer songs that are massive hits than having ten mediocre ones.*

*Don't approach record labels. Purely because A&R love to discover new bands. If you are a really good band, rehearsed, you're tight, you have great songs and you've built a fan base in your home town or city, then the industry will come to you. Because word will get back to record labels. Nothing can be kept secret. The music industry is so well connected it's impossible for record labels to not hear about bands that are creating a buzz. It's always more exciting for the A&R to discover a band after being tipped by a contact than for them to deal with bands or managers who keep calling labels asking us to hear their demo. That's because inexperienced bands or managers tend to blanket bomb the industry, by going to everyone, thinking it's the best thing to do. And then calling up the A&R office every five mins only makes you look unprofessional. I don't know anyone who has ever been signed doing that. The flip side is that it's always better for a band when the A&R person approaches them.*

*No, it's always better for a band to focus on playing their home town, creating a vibe or a buzz.*

## Mark Palmer: RoadRunner

*I broke into A&R by default more than anything else. My first job was at Music for Nations back in the 80s when the whole thrash thing was going on. And back then the label was very small with around four people running the office and the A&R being taken care of by the owner Martin Hooker. Because I was so young, enthusiastic and willing he saw an opportunity to pass on the donkey work of listening to the demos and watching bands whilst he took care of the business side. And of course I just jumped at the chance. I then signed Onslaught and English Dogs before moving* onto a 15-month period at a major label which left me frustrated. RoadRunner then came along and again at that time it was run by two or three people and I got into the A&R side by virtue of no one else doing it.

I don't think I was one of those people born to do A&R, it just sort of happened. I guess it's one of those right place right time kind of things. A lot of current A&R have probably got the gig by starting out as local promoters, or were in bands, press, etc and build a network of contacts which led to a gig. There's no training for this kind of job. You need to have a passion and dedication for the music. Have very good ears and be prepared to spend a lot of time seeing shitty bands in shitty venues where eventually you will come across something. It is one of those jobs that can be very kind of lonely in a way. A lot of A&R at major labels can go through very long periods where they don't sign any acts because there aren't that many out there that a label is prepared to invest in. And you can be at a job for years and years, at a major, without any kind of success. It's less so at independents though.

The really frustrating part about A&R is that you can have this passion, this excitement and vision for a band where you go in, sign them up and make a record, find the right studio and producer, etc, etc and when it's done you hand it over to the rest of your team and that's it. You lose all control from that point, and that's when the record's out there and it starts getting bad reviews, or you find it's not getting on the radio or whatever. That's when it starts to hurt because you have no control whatsoever to do anything about it. And this can eat into your confidence. You've had this band which is like your baby, with all the excitement thinking you have delivered a great record, and of course not everyone's taste is in line with the public's or maybe it's not that band's time. And that kind of thing happens a lot to A&R guys. So, A&R is a tough thing to get into and is even tougher to get successful at.

We probably get 25 to 30 unsolicited demos every week. Not just from the UK but the rest of the world. Then we get tons of emails from bands asking us to check out their websites or gigs. But you will rarely find a great band from an unsolicited demo. Most of the time the acts that are worth following up on are the ones who have been recommended to you by either an agent, promoter or a journalist you happen to know. That's the way you tend to find the bands you want to sign. These are the bands out there that are already creating the buzz and the ones we will follow up on.

*Personally I hate listening to bands on Myspace. I prefer to have the CD to put on when I please and listen to it on a proper stereo. The great thing about websites is that it opens up the band's music to everyone, but it also means there's a ridiculous amount of choice out there too. And 95 per cent of bands out there aren't very good. Or not worth going anywhere near signing. So whilst you are investing a lot more time trawling through websites, ultimately you end up with a similar sort of hit rate in signing bands as you did before technology came along. But I do think it's great from a band's point of view. The bands that are really active have their heads screwed on. They are out there playing shows, getting their name into the press and media, which gives them the chance to get noticed.*

*When it comes to signing bands they have to have great songs. I also look to make sure they are gigging regularly. Because if they are not then they are probably just one of those bands who sit on their arses thinking the world is going to come to them and they don't have to get out there, work and do their job. Image helps, or if they look great – even if it's a horrible thing to say that's the reality. And you like to see a structure around them. It's good if they have a manager in place as this helps with building a profile. Sending out press info, booking gigs, thinking about the next stage in their careers, planning ahead with recordings and making videos all go into showing the world professionalism. I would say to any band that unless you are really dedicated to making it happen, don't even bother, it's all or nothing. It's all in your attitude. Being in a band takes a huge sacrifice. It's not easy but then it isn't supposed to be. That's what the job is about. And it is a job. Even if it's all against you, you still have Friday, Saturday and Sunday of every month to get out there and play shows.*

*People ask me all the time why it seems American bands tend to deliver better live shows. Well, the American bands are better. They tend to have the right kind of attitude. America is this huge country and you have unsigned bands going out playing loads of shows across the States. When you see a young American band on stage they look as though they know what they need to do, to perform, to project themselves, to connect with the audience and entertain the crowd. And that kind of attitude only comes from constantly gigging and playing shows. It's really unfortunate because we invented this. We gave music to the world. But British bands do tend to underestimate the importance of the work involved, and the dedication and passion needed to make it.*

Lastly I'm going to introduce you to Andy McIntyre. I worked with Andy a few years ago and found him to be one of the best A&R men in the world. His knowledge, passion, care and understanding, along with vast experience not only in A&R but for bands and music in general, make this section of the book a god damn privilege to include him. What Andy has written is in itself a masterclass on A&R and I'm very happy to reproduce it here. Over to Andy now to end this chapter with style and grace, and for all the kids, an informative and educational account of the A&R world...

## Andy McIntyre

*'How many A&R men does it take to change a lightbulb?' 'I don't know, what do you think?' Arse & Rectum. Umm & Errr. Chinstroker. Gobshite. Bullsh\*t artist. Yep, being an 'A&R man' sure makes you popular. All of the above and many, many more have been hurled at everyone who's ever held the title at some point or other in their careers, and usually more than once. In A&R you are typically holding the thick end of the stick on the frontlines of any potential conflict, whether between artist and label, label and lawyer, or internally between departments within the company for which you have sold your soul and sacrificed your social life. These battles can and do occur at any time of the day or night; they don't respect weekends or public holidays, and whoever loses it's almost always the A&R guy's fault. The A&R department is mistrusted and misunderstood, lambasted and ridiculed, usually blamed when things go wrong, rarely credited when things go right. Usually the first to go in personnel shake-ups, it is also one of the most insecure jobs in an increasingly insecure industry.*

*So why on earth do we do it? What kind of person chooses to work in A&R? Who would volunteer themselves into this insane career? The answer, you may be surprised to learn, is virtually no one. Of all the A&R people I know, myself included, I can think of only one who began their road into the job with the words 'I want to be an A&R man'. For the rest of us, the road was far less clearly defined. In fact, in hindsight and with an objective perspective, very rarely do you choose this job; in most cases, this job chooses you.*

*I'd like to think that my first step on the road to A&R manager for a large independent record company was taken on 12 February 1994, with a phone call from the marketing manager at Mushroom Records offering me the glamorous position of office junior at their first-floor offices on the Kings Road in West London. In reality, it was in the back of a beaten-up white Toyota on a lonely desert road in Saudi Arabia in 1976. I was 3 years old, and a friend of my dad was driving with his knees, deliberately swerving into the sand drifts on either side of the highway to send sprays of fine sand billowing into the searing desert air. Cat Stevens'* Tuesday's Dead *from the brilliant* Teaser and the Firecat album *was blaring from the car stereo. It is my first memory, clear as if it were yesterday, and it marks the point at which I fell in love with music. That love, that almost all-consuming passion for music, is the number one prerequisite for anyone interested in a successful career in the music industry. It is what drives us, and it is what keeps us going through the long hours, the difficult negotiations, the politics and the bullsh\*t.*

*By the age of 15 my love affair with music was becoming complete. My record collection was already substantial, having helped me through those difficult pubescent years, and I'd broken my live music cherry, a band night in the hall under the local library. Already my social circle comprised chiefly young men sharing my passion, and it was within this circle that the next step on my journey was taken. Every Monday we would all rush out to buy whatever the must-have record of that week happened to be, and as soon as the school bell released us we would fly round to one of our houses to listen and learn, discuss and rate, compare and categorise our aural booty. Although I never would have guessed it at the time, these priceless sessions were preparing me with the second prerequisite for any A&R person worth their salt; the ability to verbalise the musical experience, and communicate it with infectious enthusiasm to others. Loving music is one thing, but being able to motivate others to buy a record or see a band you love is an absolutely essential skill for people working in music.*

*By 17 I was going to at least three gigs a week, making the hour-and-a-half long journey into London, getting very hot and sweaty, battered and bruised and euphoric in the mosh pit, then sprinting to catch the last train back. Acid House was crossing into the mainstream, the Stone Roses and the Happy Mondays had broken the mould and re-created music in their own image, and my passion for discovering music old and new was growing even more intense. It was time to become a player rather than a spectator.*

*Being utterly untalented as a musician I felt instead the call of the turntable, and on New Year's Eve 1989, in a church hall secretly 'obtained' for the purpose with bin-liners taped over the windows and a bucket for donations by the door, I dropped needle to wax for the first time in public. Suffice to say it was another defining career moment without my realising. The place went nuts, we didn't get shut down, and at some time around 10am on the first day of 1990 I blinked my way into the clear new decade one giant leap closer to where I am today.*

*That leap took the form of a realisation that there is nothing more humbling or exhilarating than being able to enrich other people's lives with music you love. Putting that realisation into practice, organising raves on the common land around my local area, took up the summer before college, and university was spent promoting clubs and gigs and DJing as much as studies would allow. Which was a lot.*

*By this point, and quite unbeknownst to me, the music industry already had me firmly in its sights. Having to take an unexpected year out and find work quickly, a friend already working on the merchandising side of the business called with the news that Mushroom Records were looking for an office junior, and would I like him to submit my CV. Silly question really, although perhaps oddly I had genuinely never once considered a career in music. In truth I still had no concrete idea what I wanted to be when I grew up (I still don't). However, I got an interview principally on the basis that 90 per cent of my CV consisted of clear evidence that my passion for music had taken me beyond the role of mere spectator, and after three interviews I got the phone call.*

*It only took three days at Mushroom to realise that I had found the place I wanted to be. All I had done in those three days was make coffee, answer phones, tidy up the stock cupboard and fill fax machines (it's how people used to communicate before the internet for those of you under the age of 23). But something about the place and the people really hooked me. My boss didn't know I had been to university, let alone that I was supposed to go back to finish my degree, and after only those three days I had decided he wasn't going to know. He is a man in whose immense debt I will forever be for his example, inspiration, and the fact that he didn't fire me when he eventually did find out!*

▶

*Something else happened then too, something seemingly trivial, but which marked me out to the terrible beast that is A&R as a potential victim. In tidying the stock cupboard I was entrusted the task of filing and cataloguing the master tapes that held the original, first-generation recordings of the albums we released. Mostly Australian acts at the time, these tapes had a strange and wonderful effect on me. They spoke to me. I held them in absolute reverence. Every drum beat, every guitar note, every vocal nuance performed by those bands in the studio had been faithfully and accurately transcribed in real time into the magnetic variations now held on those tapes. It was, and still is, a magical and mystical process to me, that something as complicated as the human voice, if passed through the correct equipment, can be captured in perfect fidelity onto tracks of magnetised tape, and then, after passing back through more equipment, be accurately reproduced by a vibrating cone of card.*

*If the process is what drives or excites you then perhaps a career in production beckons, but if it's the idea of it, the magic of it, the sheer mysticism that the performances encapsulated on those tapes will eventually find themselves in the homes, lives and memories of people the world over, then I'm afraid your cards are marked, and the A&R beast will hunt you down like the dog that you are.*

*Of course I still had no idea of this at the time.*

*I did finish my degree, and with silly hat obtained I returned to Mushroom, working in a similar position but directly for the head of its sister-label Infectious Records. In addition to scouting, a must for any A&R hopeful involving seeing three or four bands a night six nights a week, my first job there was to compile the royalty statements for all the acts on the roster, determining how much and when they should be paid. Never having done this before, and starting completely from scratch, I had to teach myself to read, understand and implement the often complicated royalty and accounting clauses in artist agreements. I also had to familiarise myself with our entire distribution and retail operations in order to make sure no sales were missed. I had to learn what production, promotion, marketing or other costs were recoupable and apply the recoupment to the accounts. It was a steep learning curve, in an area demanding total accuracy, and I loved doing it.*

*It taught me a lot about the business and how it operates, but it also taught me another more important lesson that serves me well to this day: A&R will only choose those people who can apply themselves enthusiastically to any area of the business. The more you understand of how the industry works, from the optimum contents of the stock cupboard of a small but growing independent label, to global corporate operations, the better an A&R person you will make.*

*Working at a growing independent label from the very bottom is a fantastic way to start out in this industry. Day to day you get to work with every department, watching and learning from the specialists as they go about the business of creating stars. I watched Ash go from playing in front of six people in the back room of a Camden pub to headlining both main stages at Glastonbury in the same year; I watched Garbage break through radio from nerdy studio project to multi-platinum global headliners; I watched Peter André battle his way through the melée of the mid-90s pop maelstrom to come out firmly on top; I watched all the successes, and all the failures, contributing in my way to both, but most importantly learning all the time. This learning curve is perhaps the most important step on the road to a successful A&R career. In dealing every day with artists, managers and lawyers, you need to have a deep and grounded understanding of every aspect of the business as it affects them, because you never know what you're going to be asked.*

*Almost as important as what you learn is who you learn from. Ask most successful executives and they will tell you who their mentor was or is. I was incredibly fortunate to serve under two fantastic bosses during the ten years I was at Mushroom, and it was the second of these, himself a very highly regarded A&R man in his previous incarnation at a major, who spotted my potential and began guiding me down the path he himself had already taken. It was with a seemingly innocuous phrase that my fate was sealed: 'You've got good ears Andy, why don't you cut this single.' Hooked. The b\*stard. 'You've got good ears.' It's such an odd thing to tell someone. You certainly wouldn't use it as a chat-up line, nor would you use it to describe a friend's new-born baby. It's not really a phrase you'd use on meeting an old acquaintance after a long time apart, and I'm certain no witness statement has ever included the line in describing a suspect. It is, however, absolutely essential to have them in order to do what we do.*

▶

*Now you may not know this, but having good ears in the context of A&R is really saying two things, both very different, and both very important. First, it's saying you have the ability to hear whether something will translate, whether it has the potential for commercial success (however that is defined). Second, it's a comment on your technical hearing ability: can you listen to a mix and tell whether the guitars are too loud, or the vocal too effected, or that the balance is right or wrong, or are there any phasing issues around the edit that's just been done? There is some debate as to whether these 'good ears' are acquired or learned, a sort of 'nature versus nurture' argument if you will. My feeling is that there is an element of predetermination, that some people are born with better ears than others, however this nascent talent needs to be nurtured and developed, trained and focused.*

*It is for this reason that I pinpoint the start of my journey all the way back in that car in Saudi; literally ever since I can remember, and quite unconsciously, I have been an A&R-man-in-training. By constantly listening to music of as many genres and styles as possible, by going to as many gigs as possible, by promoting and DJing as much as possible, by talking and listening to people about music my entire life, whatever talent there was in my ears has been honed and primed to be able to do what I do, and it's a process that is still ongoing.*

*After ten years with the Mushroom Group of Companies it was finally time to move on, so I left my job as A&R manager for Infectious Records. Having then spent a year as a freelance consultant working with managers of young acts and small labels I was offered and gladly accepted the role of A&R manager at Eagle Rock Entertainment, also an independent label, but a different beast entirely from Mushroom. Instead of working new and developing acts, Eagle specialises in the other end of the market, and I am privileged to work with a roster of artists who have had immense success over many decades, often defining the genres in which they excel. The likes of John Mayall, Gary Moore, Alice Cooper, Shane MacGowan, Willy DeVille, Testament, Candy Dulfer, and the other artists with whom I work provide a whole new set of challenges and experiences, and my learning curve took another steep incline upwards. Also, being somewhat larger than Mushroom, the other set of skills essential to any prospective A&R person are constantly being tested and refined at Eagle; those skills which can be broadly grouped under the term 'political'.*

*In addition to having good ears and a solid understanding of the business, good A&R involves being able to communicate and mediate effectively between many different people. Once you've discovered a band you want to work with you have to be able to sell your label to them as the best home they could possibly have to release their records from, or to put their songs with if you're in publishing. You also need to be able to sell the band to your colleagues, infecting them with your enthusiasm for the act. You need to negotiate the broader points of the record deal with the act, their management and legal team, and mediate the completion of the longform agreement with your own lawyers. You need to be able to find the right team to make the records, negotiate their deals and help smooth and resolve any disagreements during the record-making process (and believe me there are many!). You need to be able to negotiate a reasonable allocation of your label's resources to be devoted to working your band in terms of people's time and the company's money, and manage the relationship between act and label. You need to mediate with the manager between the often conflicting demands for the band's time from agents, PRs, recording schedules and families.*

*In short, and in the words of the marvellous Vanilla Ice, if there is a problem, yo, you solve it. It is a highly demanding and difficult job requiring patience, tact, diplomacy and finesse, and the stakes are high; people's dreams and livelihoods are at stake.*

*This is why A&Rs are so roundly misunderstood both within the industry and outside it. It's not just about signing bands. If you're doing your job well you become almost invisible. When you're really on top of your game and everything is running smoothly, the artists you're signing are happy and successful, the relationship between artist and label is calm and effective, when the resources needed to do the job of making, promoting and selling records are available in proportion to their need, and when your catalogue is being exploited to its maximum potential, it can appear to those around you that you're not really doing very much.*

*However, when there are problems or conflicts, it's you that has to step swiftly and fearlessly into the breach, to take the flack from all directions, to dig around in the muck until you've identified the problem and then deal with it. You roll with the punches, you take the abuse, you juggle with*

▶

*the elements 15 at a time until a resolution is reached, then you dust yourself off and get ready for the next call-up, any time, day or night.*

*So those are the characteristics and skills that will mark you out as a potential A&R victim. An all-consuming love of music that goes beyond the passive to the active. An ability to communicate that passion effectively. A hunger and ability to learn as much as possible about music and the music business. Surrounding yourself with inspirational mentors. Good ears. A full palette of diplomatic skills. Thick skin and a good sense of humour. It really is a f\*cking brilliant job, and I wouldn't do anything else for all the rice in China. Think you've got what it takes? If so, and if you're lucky, maybe the A&R beast will hunt you down, bite you on the arse and never let you go.*

*If you're lucky.*

# The Publishing Company

The music publisher's role is essentially to seek out and exploit songs. Publishers are always hungry for new talent and with the never-ending slue of manufactured pop bands they need a never-ending supply of hit songs. Whether you are a band or a songwriter, approaching a publisher is part of your overall game plan. In certain circumstances bands/songwriters are able to attain an advance from publishers to record master demos. These recordings are then used to help secure a record deal. It also shows from the publisher's side that they believe in you and will develop the songwriter/band with the help of master quality recordings. If you are just a songwriter with no aspirations of performing live you will have a hard time to get a recording artist to sing one of your songs unless you are signed to a publishing company.

The difference between a publishing and a record company is that record labels are looking more or less for the finished product, where as the publishing company is looking for songs. And whilst you should always submit your best tracks, unless the recording is really terrible, in which case do it again, the publishing company A&R can hear a good song when it's played. That sounds like an old cliché to me but it's true. More can be done with a song than can be done with a band. You can break songs up, chop them around and find something in there than can lead to another direction. With a bad band, well they are doomed.

## ESTABLISHING YOURSELF AS A SONGWRITER

The style of music you write may be fashionable now, but as we all know fashions change very quickly. So don't hold on to songs. You may have just written something that's perfect for what a publisher is looking for. And whilst the odds are always against you the song can't do much good sitting there on your hard drive. From a band perspective the likelihood of getting a publisher to seek a record deal is no guarantee, but it can happen. However, it doesn't automatically mean that if you sign to EMI Publishing then you would sign to EMI Records, or any other label for that matter. At the very least it will confirm you have a good chance of establishing yourself as a good songwriter. And that's the entire point here.

So the good news is that music publishers do look for new songwriters: quality and cutting edge songwriters are the key ingredients to their publishing empire. The publisher's role is to ensure songwriters are paid for the use of their music by licensing, promoting, managing and safeguarding the copyright and royalties of their work. In other words they should seek to generate income from everything but straight sales in shops. In return, a songwriter assigns the publishing rights of their material, which entitles the publisher to print copies of the song for sale, and to promote the song to record companies and artists. Publishers will also license the songs to be performed by other artists once permission has been granted and then administer the commission.

## Do you need to be a performer?

As a songwriter you are not required to be a current performer. A former artist such as Cathy Dennis (Kylie Minogue's greatest hits) is an example of a previous artist enjoying songwriting as a career. However, breaking into the publishing world is still a difficult mission. It is very competitive with the only requirement being top quality songwriting. You are after all up against the best songwriters in the world. So when submitting your material make sure it really is the best stuff you have. Otherwise you will not find it any easier to get that elusive deal as a performer. The upside to this is that if you have had enough of running around the UK in the back of the trusty old transit van and wish to just focus on writing and recording, then the publishing route may be more favourable.

## WHAT PUBLISHING COMPANIES DO

Whilst there are independent and smaller publishers who exist to publish their own acts, most major publishing companies are owned by the same corporations that own the major record labels. Record companies may sign bands for limited periods, but the publishers can retain, control and sell the rights for decades or for the entire life of the copyright. The reason for this is that songs are eternal. With the digital age songs are now more required than ever for use in movies, TV and commercials. You may think it's unreasonable to sign away the rights to your songs for their copyright life, but if in five years you have a song placed on a Hollywood blockbuster movie, then you won't be too unhappy when that nice royalty cheque comes through the door. It may just be enough to make you choke on your cornflakes.

Aside from seeking new talent a publisher will spend most of their working time controlling the use of their copyrights, collecting royalties, securing synchronisation licences and generally exposing the writer's talents. The MCPS (Mechanical Copyright Protection Society) (in the UK) is the most likely used agency for collecting royalties. (See Chapter 6 for more on the role of MCPS and PRS.) Both companies were established to represent publishers, songwriters and artists to protect their rights, along with negotiating agreements with third parties who seek to use recordings on CDs and other media.

## PUBLISHING RIGHTS

Publishing rights are the rights to a song. Once you have written a song, you own the publishing and copyright. The rights to the song you have written automatically belong to the author or writer.

However, when it comes to a publishing deal things do change. Publishing can be dividied into two halves. One is called the **writer's share** and the other the **publisher's share** which you as a writer own as well. When you sign a publishing deal this definition changes. You then give up some of the publishing rights, which is normally half or all of the Publisher's share in exchange for an advance from the music publisher. Deals will always vary so it is even more important to get legal advice, and in some circumstances an accountant can come in handy to show you real projections of income based on the various splits and possible income streams.

## Royalities

Each time a song gets played on the radio, appears on an album, is used on TV or in the movies, is sold as sheet music or books, is used in video games and as is the case now as a ring tone, the song generates money for the writer or writers. Each time this happens a royalty is accrued which goes to the publishing company and on to the writer minus the publisher's share. The royalty rates will vary for each of these sources of income and should range from anything from 50 to 75 per cent in the artist's favour.

## THE PUBLISHER'S ROLE IN RECORD DEALS

Some artists are able to secure a publishing deal before a recording deal. This generally tends to be more singer/songwriter types than full blown bands. James Blunt was signed to EMI Publishing for three years before his success came. He didn't just womble off his tank singing *You're Beautiful* straight into a record deal and world success. EMI developed him and spent truckloads of money over time placing him in studios to hone his sound and work with different songwriters before any music was released.

If a publisher has belief in a singer-songwriter or artists they can get proactive in helping secure a record contract. This tends to be through financing a set number of master quality studio recordings, sometimes a video, to pitch to a record label. The publisher will guarantee a specific amount of finance to record master quality tracks and, if a recording artist agreement is secured, will receive a production or executive producer royalty of one to three per cent under the agreement.

Publishers may go even further and finance the entire album to license or sell to a record label. In this instance the publisher will be entitled to royalty points from the record company and will recoup the recording costs. This can be a rare occurrence, but as the music industry changes and record and publishing companies change their business models this kind of deal will happen more often.

## APPROACHING THE PUBLISHER

Approaching a music publisher is the same as approaching everyone else in the music industry. They have an A&R department with similar jobs for seeking new talent. Again, make sure you do some research on the publisher before you approach them. Sending punk rock to a classical division would only make you look very unprofessional and your material being sent back. As always it will be a difficult road if you are not an established writer or performer, but keep your feet on the ground and make sure you present your very best material. As a songwriter they will want to know that you are prolific. That's not to say you should mention you have over 100 songs, as the likelihood is that they will think the quality is bound to be suspect.

### Collaborative writing

If you write in collaboration with someone else make sure you have an agreement on all the songwriting splits to avoid any future dispute. It's always easy to get caught up in the you against the world syndrome, but relationships can change very quickly and it's worth protecting yourself. If you have an agreement and the co-writer decides he wants to jump ship and refuse you permission for his part of the song that leaves you totally sunk, unless of course you have an agreement that has been overseen by a music industry solicitor. It's always best to get the business side of a relationship sorted before the fun begins.

Make sure you have your songs available online. Sending in unsolicited demos to publishers will mostly result in rejections much like we mentioned in A&R. The best thing for a song is to get it heard by people and if they walk away whistling the tune then you have a winner. However, if you need a singer to use in the track get the best you can find. Many songs can be ruined by the wrong use of vocalists for the sake of haste. A good song will shine through, but expect your musical discovery to take a bit of time, if only to avoid disappointment and six months of depression.

## Exploitation

After a writer has signed the publishing deal and delivered the material it is part of the publishing company's job to exploit the music. This means presenting the music to record labels, managers, producers and artists in an attempt to obtain a recording contract for the copyrights held.

- Songs released on a physical format like CDs are called **mechanicals**.

- Songs that are played on the radio, TV or through a live performance are called the **performance rights**.

- Songs featured in movies and DVDs are the **synchronised rights**.

- Downloaded songs are called **digital streaming**.

These are the areas in which your songs will be exploited.

The publishing company will want you to succeed and will be active in arranging writing sessions and pitching ideas to established artists, producers and A&R guys. The business side will be explained and advised to you by your solicitor. Publishers will want the rights to all the songs you have written unless you have assigned rights to another publisher. This will be discussed and negotiated with the lawyer. Royalties are usually paid to the writer twice a year, in six-month blocks, based on the amount received by the publisher. You will receive a detailed account of all royalties accrued. You must also be allowed to audit or inspect the company's accounts at least once a year. Hopefully this will not be needed, but royalties and statements can get quite confusing especially when there is sub-licensing involved.

> **Client: singer/songwriter**
>
> *This real-life case study illustrates difficulties with publishing/co-writer agreements.*
>
> Background
>
> *The client had written some songs with a co-writer, having met through a music website. They had agreed via email to split any income from the song that either writer managed to create.*
>
> Legal problem
>
> *When attempting to sell the track online my client became embroiled in arguments and disputes with the co-writer over who had the authority to approve selling the song. This culminated in a six-month long dispute in which my client found abusive and threatening posts on various websites, causing much harm to their musical career.*
>
> Legal diagnosis
>
> *Eventually they agreed to sign a co-writer document that I drafted covering all splits and necessary approvals. If this had been done immediately after the song had been written then the problem would have been avoided.*

## PUBLISHING ADVANCES

A publisher will usually offer you a one-year deal with an option to renew your contract for up to two more years. If you are an unsigned artist, you might receive an advance of between £1,000–50,000 for what is called a **publishing development deal**. The publisher is advancing you money so that you can record high-quality demos (for your own CD, perhaps), buy some new equipment and maybe pay some living expenses so you can concentrate on getting your record deal.

However, many artists/bands elect to hold off on making a publishing deal until they first secure a record deal. The reason is that, as a signed artist, you can command a much higher advance. Publishers are willing to pay a premium for an act that is already signed and supported by a major label. Many signed bands can secure up to £100,000 for their first album, and 'buzz bands' can attract as much as £200,000 or more.

If you are a songwriter who is not an artist, or without a proven track record, the advance can usually be around £3,000 or upwards of £10,000 unless you have songs already placed with established acts and are willing to include those songs in your deal. Then, the advance could be more lucrative because the publisher now sees potential royalties from which to recoup.

## A GUIDE TO MUSIC PUBLISHING TERMINOLOGY

There's no doubt that the area of publishing is a detailed and often confusing part of the industry. With so many sources of income and rights involved I have to spend a lot of time explaining the numerous elements to clients. So I've put together a glossary of terms with some legal terminology explained by Elliot Chalmers of **www.musiclawadvice.co.uk**

**Administration** The supervising for a fee (generally a percentage of income), usually by a major music publisher, of a smaller music publisher's financial and copyright matters regarding one or more songs or an entire catalogue. The administrator does not necessarily own a share of the copyright, although one co-publisher could administer another co-publisher's share.

**Advance** The payment in advance of royalties to be earned in the future, and recouped by offsetting those future earned royalties against the money advanced. Advances are usually non-refundable.

**Audio/visual work** An industry term for film, television or any other visual production.

**Assignment of copyright** The transfer of ownership of a copyright from one party to another, which must be in writing to be effective.

**Audit clause** An important clause in any agreement between a songwriter and a publisher, or any business agent, that allows the songwriter the right to have access to the publisher's books and records (usually once a year), so that the songwriter can determine the accuracy of the publisher's accounting practices.

**Author** The creator of 'intellectual property' such as literary, musical and dramatic works; choreography; pictorial, graphic and sculptural works; audio/visual works and sound recordings. Therefore the word author can denote composer, lyricist, record producer, choreographer, artist, photographer, writer or other creator (see '**work made for hire**').

**Background music** Music used (other than as feature or theme music) that creates mood and supports the spoken dialogue of a radio programme or visual action of an audio/visual work.

**Blanket licence** For an annual fee, radio and television stations, public broadcasters, cable stations, universities, restaurants, programmed music services, etc, can acquire a 'blanket licence' from a performing rights organisation. This licence gives them the right to perform every piece of music contained in the respective repertoire as often as they wish during the term of the licence.

**Catalog(ue)** The most commonly used word in reference to the collection of songs owned by a publisher/songwriter.

**Common information system (CIS)** A collection of global databases which are used as sources of documentation for royalty distributions by CISAC members.

**Composers** The men and women who create musical compositions for motion pictures and other audio/visual works, or the creators of classical music compositions.

**Compulsory mechanical licence** A licence provided by the Copyright Law allowing anyone to record a song that has previously been commercially recorded with authorisation.

**Controlled composition** A composition written or co-written by the recording artist (and sometimes the producer per the artist contract) under an exclusive recording agreement. Typically, the recording company will pay 75 per cent of the minimum statutory rate on only ten cuts per CD and two cuts per single, regardless of the actual number of sides or length of the composition(s).

**Copyright** The exclusive right, granted by law for a stated period, usually until 70 years after the death of the surviving author of the work, to make, dispose of, and otherwise control copies of literary, musical, dramatic, pictorial and other copyrightable works.

**Cue sheet** A listing of the music used in a television programme or motion picture by title, composer, publisher, timing and type of usage (e.g, background, feature, theme) usually prepared by the producer of the programme or film.

**Derivative work** A work derived from another work, such as a translation, musical arrangement, sound recording, or motion picture version.

**Exclusive rights** The right of a copyright owner to exclusively authorise recording, performance, dramatisation or other uses of their works, as set forth in the Copyright Act.

**Exclusive songwriter agreement** A contract between a publisher and a songwriter in which the songwriter assigns all songs written during the term of the contract to the publisher in return for a percentage of royalty income. Such an agreement usually involves advances paid by the publisher to the songwriter.

**Grand rights** The term used to describe 'dramatic' performing rights. This would cover performances of musicals.

**Infringement** A violation of the exclusive rights granted by the copyright law to a copyright owner.

**Lead sheet** A hand-made (usually) reproduction on paper of a newly-written song.

**Library** A collection of musical compositions that are licensed by the publisher or administrator for use as background, theme, or score music, on radio, broadcast and cable television, films, or video productions.

**Licence** A licence is a grant to a 'user' permitting use of a copyright for any of the following:

1. Mechanical (records, tapes, CDs).

2. Non-dramatic performance (public performance of a song over radio/TV/club/hotel/concerts).

3. Grand rights (dramatic performance of a musical work, musical comedy, play, opera, operetta, or ballet).

4. Synchronisation (the use of a musical composition on the soundtrack of an audio/visual work for theatrical exhibition or television).

5. Print (sheet music, folios, songbooks or other printed editions. The grant is usually made for a specified period of time and for a designated territory).

6. Commercial (the use of a musical composition as part of an advertisement).

**Mechanical licence** The license issued by a publisher or their agent, usually to a record company, granting the record company the right to record and release a specific composition at an agreed-upon fee per unit manufactured and sold.

**Performing rights organisation** An association or corporation that licenses the public performance of non-dramatic musical works on behalf of the copyright owners, such as the American Society of Composers, Authors, and Publishers. These performing rights organisations issue licences to users of publicly performed, non-dramatic music for a fee, and then pay performing rights royalties to the publishers and songwriters of the performed works.

**Public domain** Refers to the status of a work having no copyright protection and, therefore, belonging to the world. When a work is 'in' or has 'fallen into' the public domain it means it is available for unrestricted use by anyone.

**Sampling** When sound bytes are removed electronically from a master recording and through technological imitation placed within the context of another composition. The length of the bytes can be limitless, and can contain lyric and music in combination or in part from any segment of the score. Depending upon the length of the bytes and how they are used, unauthorised sampling could be held to be a copyright infringement of the sound recording from which they were taken and from the musical work they first appeared in.

**Score** The music that is used in synchronisation with an audio/visual work, or the body of music composed for a dramatic-musical work.

**Single song assignment** A contract between a publisher and songwriter(s) where the songwriter assigns to the publisher the copyright in one particular song in return for a percentage of royalty income. Sometimes referred to as a 'one-off' contract.

**Sound recording** The copyrighted musical work that results from the fixation of sounds onto a phonorecord.

**Source licence** In performing rights, a licence granted by the copyright owner to the person, producer or organisation being licensed to record or distribute the work (e.g. in a taped programme), so that the performance of the recorded work needs no further licence.

**Split publishing** When the publishing rights in a song are held by more than one publisher. Each of the several publishers is called a 'co-publisher'.

**Sub-publishing** A contractual arrangement between an original publisher of a song and a foreign publisher to handle the exploitation, licensing and collection for the song in the foreign publisher's territory.

**Synchronisation right** The exclusive right of a copyright owner, granted by the Copyright Act, to authorise the recording of a musical work onto the soundtrack of an audio/visual work. The song is synchronised with images on the screen, hence the name.

**Synchronisation royalties** The amount of money earned by the publisher (and, consequently, divided with the songwriter) for the use of a song for which a synchronisation licence has been issued.

**Work made for hire** A work prepared by an employee within the scope of his/her employment, or a work specially ordered or commissioned for use by another person in accordance with a written document as a contribution to a collective work, motion picture, audio/visual and other certain types of works.

# What You Need to Know About Management

Before we go into depth regarding what managers are for and what to expect from them, having a good manager in place is a must for any band wanting a professional career playing music. They are the conduit between the band and the business world of the music industry. A good manager frees the band up to focus on writing new songs and playing live. They need to have the same vision as the band and trust is the single most important aspect in this relationship. I say relationship, but I really mean professional relationship. There has to be trust in the business and financial affairs along with trust that they are doing the best job on behalf of the band all the time. Yes, there are stories out there from the old days where management would tie the band into deals of the worst kind. In this day and age it is rare for these kinds of things to happen, but there are issues that I will point out that you should be aware of. Firstly I want to get it from the horse's mouth from a music industry manager of 30 years' standing who in my opinion really shows what they can do for a band. Especially against all the odds.

## MEET A MANAGER

Rod Smallwood has been the manager of Iron Maiden since 1979 when the band was beginning to emerge from London's East End. Smallwood and Maiden have gone on to typify what a rock band actually stand for and are a great example of getting it right, with integrity, belief, great songs, great live stage shows and maximising how important merchandise can be to a band. Maiden built their fan base through constantly touring and playing without the support of radio, including in the USA. This in itself proves the calibre of the band and emphasises all the facets a young band should be aware off. I sat down with Rod at the office of Phantom Music to discuss the relationship a band and their manager should have. And for me he covered everything that needed to be said…

### What should a band look for in a new manager and what should a manger look for in a band?

I think for most successful bands the relationship with a good manager is historically pretty key. Most big bands have a good manager but these are not always in place at the beginning, although in the case of Maiden I was their first manager as Steve Harris had the sense to wait until he found what he thought was the right situation for him. Quite often young bands get friends to do it in the beginning and when this starts to not work as is the case more often than not – they will start to look around or the record company will suggest they find someone more suited and experienced. Some young managers will continue with the band and sometimes that works and sometimes that doesn't, as it's very much down to the ability of the individual. So the main thing to do, as continuity is very important in a career, is to be very careful who you elect as your manager in the first place.

If you are going to have a friend manage you make it clear from the beginning that if it develops into a serious career, and they show they can develop the progress of the band and keep abreast and ahead of it in terms of where the band want to be business-wise and creatively, then you will look at doing a contract with them – but not before you are sure they can handle it. Be very clear that this is a trial period. Ideally though try to find the right sort of manager in the first place. And that's really about the style and genre of the band. I deal with heavy rock and I wouldn't deal with anything else. I certainly wouldn't want to deal with, say, a pop band or bands of that ilk. I wouldn't be much use, as I don't enjoy that style of music very much, so it would be a pointless exercise, and secondly I don't have the contacts in that area so it wouldn't be something I would want to pursue.

So make sure you get a manager in your musical genre, as that will make life easier and they will understand what you are trying to achieve much more. Maybe they have had past success, and that would show they have the contacts and experience to know how to manage you. Do whatever you can to check out a potential manager's background and experience, but if you can't do that then talk to them extensively. Ask questions about the genre you are in, the music, bands they have worked with, and see if you feel you can trust them. Quite often if you look someone in the eye you can actually feel if they are someone you can trust or not. Use your instinct, it is usually correct. And have a few drinks with them. When people have a few drinks they tend to get closer to their real selves!

My next question concerned what a manager should bring to the table. Should they have a plan already formed, should the band have the plan or should it be a two-way discussion?

### Should the band sign a management contract straight away or should there be a period of grace to see how things develop?

That depends on the manager. At the end of the day management and artists is a trust relationship. A manager should initially be prepared to show how they work and the initial phase of the relationship is trust. But there are two sides to this. From a manager's point of view there is nothing worse than taking a band on, developing them to a great extent and then doing the contract only to have a lawyer in one of the big companies decimate the deal. A good manager will make sure any artist would go to a good music business lawyer of which there are quite a number in London and elsewhere now. Issues like perpetual commission, which from a manager's viewpoint is very key, will come up and some lawyers will try to cut commission down to net deals. I would never work on a net deal because it's a conflict. Why should it be in my financial interest to, say, convince the band to use a cheap PA and a shitty lightshow to save money so I can commission more? I wouldn't do it but you can see how this can potentially be a conflict.

The trouble with trial periods from a manager's point of view is that if you do work on a trust basis, are successful and what you implement works, you can then get penalised for it. But then a band shouldn't go into a five-year contract, which is fairly standard, until they feel sure they have made the right choice. So probably from experience I would say get immediate legal advice and sit down with the manager and lawyer and do a heads of agreement based on a trial period with certain terms, which become the basis of the terms on the real contract when executed. There's nothing worse for a manager than to be working your balls off and then to be killed on the deal. It happens quite a lot. I think the days of the shark manager are over as it's a very professional business nowadays. And you really don't want to reduce the enthusiasm of the manager by the lawyer castrating them on the deal.

There are some very good points for bands to understand there and I think it's refreshing to get this kind of honesty. The conversation continued…

### What do you look for in a band?

For me it's always been about live performance. This is the key. They have to be a very, very good live band. Following that obviously is the songs. Image is important to an extent, musicianship is important too. You may have three members of the band who can cut it and one can't. For things to progress that would have to change at some point. And that is always very difficult for a band to handle, especially if they are friends. But it's a reality of their career.

### In today's climate using digital technology would you be focused on fighting for a deal, or would you try to build a fan base?

It's horses for courses. It depends on how developed the band is. Some bands might come to you when they have done the basic touring and built the fan base, but most experienced managers will certainly have A&R contacts who they can get down to see the band live, even if they are not looking for a deal at that point. Even though it was a long time ago with Maiden the principles are still pretty much the same for rock bands. We were doing gigs to build up the following for about four months before I got any A&R to come down. That wasn't because the band weren't ready to be looked at, it was because I wanted to build a following to show it would work. If you can show that it works in the East End of London then it will work in London, and will work in England, then will work in Europe and worldwide because metal is very much a worldwide phenomenon. The deal will always be that much better if you can show the record company that it's working and people are coming and getting into the band. And the bigger the following obviously the better. So with Maiden what I did was book them into the Marquee Club in Soho with a capacity of 700. We sold it out and the record company came down to the first show to a rammed club and people going completely nuts. The label got it straight away and immediately wanted to do a deal. If I had brought them down four months earlier, playing to 40 people at the Ruskin Arms in the East End, the performance wouldn't have been a lot different but the impact of the performance on the label would have been totally different. If you are a good live band you will build the following if you get out and play whenever you can.

### How has the internet affected your day-to-day working life?

I haven't looked to sign any bands myself really since the internet kicked in. I am happy now devoting all my attention to Maiden. But especially over the last few years with things like YouTube coming along it can make a big difference. So in terms of signing a band I would use it to maximise web presence. Material should be placed on there in as many appropriate places as possible. I wouldn't put eight songs on a website, I would choose the four best tracks with one you could download and keep, the others streamed. I would do a cheap video as everyone has movie cameras now. I would still though concentrate on the live aspect, place posters all over the gig and let people take them away. It's contact with the band and I think the audience/band contact is really important. And this you can do from an early stage. Try to get email addresses so you can circulate information to the fans. We all know that with a good website you can actually create a following quite quickly through the web. One of the problems with it though is it's not as focused as a regional live build up. But it all helps with getting the message across. As time goes on selling records becomes less important to a band in terms of income, so the live performance is key, backed up by merchandising. Record sales are down so much and with all the deductions that most deals have with promotion, marketing, tour support, etc, at the end of the day if you ever recoup you are doing exceptionally well. Obviously some bands do, but a lot more don't.

### And lastly, what advice would you give to a young band?

I think trust between band and manager is a very important thing. Being able to move things quickly and being trusted by the band to make the decisions needed is very important. If the label asks me about something I can say either a yes or no without asking four or five people. It's very good for a band to have a leader, which obviously Maiden have always had with Steve (Harris, Maiden bass player) because then the communication between band and manager is generally through one person. Bands as democracies are hard to make function smoothly. You can't have five people deciding what to do, as you would never get anywhere. So, the decision-making process is very important. The trust level myself and Maiden have enjoyed for many many years has been key and the decision-making process has always been very good. And also fast so opportunities are not missed.

Other things to be aware include having a certain amount of discipline. Whilst it's rock and roll it's not ideal if you're fucked up at every gig! You have to take care of yourselves on the road, as things can be quite brutal. Also it's good to work as a team. Teamwork is key. We have always tried to keep a good team together. Our agent John Jackson has been with us since 1979, as has our sound engineer and Steve's bass tech. Our production guy has been with us since 1980, our merchandiser since 1982. We built a good team based on professionalism and on trust and again can move very quickly. And as the team all tend to get on very well it makes it more fun... and let's face it, at the end of the day that's very important too!

The key points for me from our conversation are that young bands need to focus on the live aspects, more of which we will cover later. I wanted to convey the discussion like Rod was sitting down and speaking with you. All the points to me were valid so take it on board.

## DO YOU NEED MANAGEMENT?

For most bands slogging their guts out on the toilet gig circuits of the UK, gaining management can be quite flattering. And I'm talking about the kind of management who are successful and can be a valuable asset to the band's career. It's been written that this could be your first taste of success but that to me is bogus. Your first taste is in getting a fan base who are going wild at your gigs, after all this is what has attracted a manager to you in the first place as they can see the money signs. So, whilst it's a positive step for you, remember that you are the one with the power.

Nobody is more important than the band. At this stage you will have to relinquish some control. For instance, up to that point you are in charge of booking your own gigs, and you may be happy for someone else to come in and take control. Most management deals will involve the management company having sole and exclusive rights to exploit you as a band/artist. This means that only they can book your gigs and arrange promotional events. This may suit some acts, but if you have been booking your own gigs and all of a sudden the management go in and get heavy, demanding more money or better slots, this only tends to peeve the people who up to this point have supported you. And this is where you tend to lose your innocence. A good manager however should honour the support you have gained and, if they need to get heavy, they should do so with bigger venues you have yet to play.

- Managers become necessary once you've got a record deal and you need an advocate to represent your interests at the different departments of a record company. They help to coordinate efforts and get maximum results at radio, retail and publicity. Many labels will want an artist to have a high-powered manager before a record is released and will often recommend top managers.

- Managers can also help in shopping for a record deal, but only if they have the connections to get your music to the right people. It's not impossible, but friends, family members, or acquaintances with no music industry experience usually aren't going to be able to get through locked industry doors, and will probably be in over their heads even if they can get through.

● Good managers help the artist assemble a competent team of professionals to handle various aspects of the artist's career, including a lawyer, a business manager (for financial affairs), a booking agent (for live performances), a merchandising company (for t-shirt sales, etc) and more. Experience counts for a lot when it comes to choosing a manager.

## Finding the right manager

So when it comes to discussing these issues it's important you feel comfortable with the outcome. If you are presented with a contract the first thing you do is get legal advice. Never ever feel pressurised into signing anything or fear losing any potential manager because of this. Stay well clear of anyone who makes you feel uncomfortable. You must find out as much as you can about potential managers. Do they belong to a bigger company? If so, what other bands do they have? If they are a lone manager find out who they are currently representing or who they have represented. Also, how current are they? Some people think because there were involved in the music industry 20 years ago, you may be the band they are coming out of retirement for. I've seen this happen and generally they are 20 years out of date.

If the manager is current then find out how long they have been in business for, along with the kind of deals they have been involved with. All good managers will be happy to sit down and go over their history. After all, what is there to hide? Again, there is no hard and fast rule about when you should sign a management contract as it all depends on how fast your career is moving. Some companies have asked for a fee upfront – do not *ever* do this. No band should ever pay a manager any kind of payment to get managed and if you get this offered always say *no*! And then email me and Elliot at The Rock and Roll Times so we can expose them for the charlatans they are, ok? Good.

## AT WHAT POINT SHOULD I GET A MANAGER?

Most of the manager's duties and responsibilities come into play once an artist is generating income – especially through a record company association, but also for active local and regional artists who are touring and selling product on their own. Therefore, many people think it isn't really necessary to have a manager until there is an income-producing career to 'manage'.

One exception is the manager who can help you obtain a record deal. The right manager for this task can be hard to find, and must be carefully chosen. You don't want to get tied up in complicated legal contracts with inexperienced managers who will need to be replaced once a record deal comes along.

Most managers will take between 10 and 20 per cent of an artist's gross income – including record royalties, publishing income, and touring and merchandising income. There will sometimes be a 'sunset clause', i.e. a declining scale of payments due to the manager over a few years should you decide to fire or part ways with him or her.

---

### Client: solo artist

#### A Real-life scenario

Background

*The client had been signed to a management company for two years and had three years left on his deal.*

Legal problem

*The client had signed a recording deal in the first year of his management term that he had got through a contact. His management deal had not been looked at by a lawyer when he signed and he found that the management company were due income from the recording deal that they had nothing to do with. Subsequently the management company have made money despite doing nothing at all.*

Legal diagnosis

*The artist should have made sure the management contract stated that their commission could only come from work actually procured by them as well as having option periods of no more than 18 months allowing him to terminate on grounds of non-performance.*

These are negotiable points, and many nuances and technicalities are involved. You should always have an experienced music business attorney (not your Uncle Bob, the divorce attorney) review any management contract.

## MANAGEMENT DEALS: WHAT TO LOOK OUT FOR

The section that follows, concerning the legalese and terms of a management contract, has been overseen by Elliot Chalmers who runs Independent Music Law Advice and specialises in representing new bands and young labels. He's also the lawyer for The Rock and Roll Times. He's also the guy who keeps me out of trouble.

What follows now are brief examples of what you can expect in a standard management contract.

Once you are satisfied that the management company might be right for you then you can look at the deal. Below are some examples of common management deal clauses that you should look out for, with a comment on what they might mean and how they will affect you as an artist. Like all our advice in this book it is important to be aware that all contracts are individual to the band itself, and always require expert advice when negotiating and deciding whether or not to sign.

*The term of this agreement shall be for a period commencing on this date hereof and continuing until the date … years thereafter…*

Although you might be happy that they have offered you a long-term deal of say three years, I would always advise you to shorten it to no longer than a year with an option to extend the deal. This way you are able to assess after a period of time whether the company has helped your career. This assessment will be based on the amount of exposure you have gained under them, and obviously how close you feel you are to getting a record deal or whether you are seeing an increase in exposure.

A simple option clause should look something like the one below:

*We shall have one irrevocable option to extend the term provided that the option will only be exercisable by us in the event that you have entered into an exclusive recording or publishing agreement approved by you during the term.*

This is another important clause, which shows that the company must aim towards arranging a record deal for you. However, it doesn't mean that however many A&R contacts a manager has that they will automatically get you signed. Nobody can guarantee that. They should though be able to utilise the contacts they do have. Many bands may come unstuck after a period of time where it's been proven that the management company has exhausted all roads to the music industry and it becomes apparent that it's in the best interests of both parties to sever ties and move on. As you can see above they must procure a *bona fide* deal in order to extend the term. Other such clauses may allow the band to terminate the contract if no deal has been found. This performance clause is vital and I always encourage it to be in any type of management deal. It is much more direct and it puts the onus on them to achieve your ultimate goal.

*We (the company) shall not be entitled to sign any agreement on your behalf and we hereby undertake not to hold ourselves out as having the right to do so.*

This is a very simple yet important clause to have in a management deal. It means that any decisions that are made about you as an artist must be approved by you first. This highlights the importance of sounding out the company and building an amicable relationship with them. Many deals may not have this clause in them, which would allow the company to involve you in events that might be more beneficial to them than you. You will want as much exposure as possible but certain methods may not suit you. You should also look out for a clause that gives power of attorney to the company. This should never be in there as it essentially allows them to sign agreements on your behalf. Not to be advised.

*The management agrees to use our best endeavours to advance, promote and develop your career as a recording artist in the music industry in accordance with your wishes and generally to render all services customarily rendered by a first class professional manager in the music industry.*

The above clause, sometimes known as engagement, seems simple enough, but is vital if you felt like the management were not performing at their best. This clause would allow you to terminate on grounds of material breach and is therefore paramount to measuring how capable they are. There are loads of things you can include in an agreement, including restricting the manager to a 'sole management' deal whereby they only manage you. There are few managers likely to desire this as it will limit their potential earnings, however if you become a major artist then you will require a committed manager who has the time to concentrate on your affairs. There should also be provisos dealing with what would happen if either party breached the contract.

*The management shall make available to you sufficient time and attention of the personal services of ... in order for him to properly provide and perform her services hereunder on a day-to-day basis.*

Sometimes known as a key man clause, this must be in the contract if you are signing to a management company or even an individual. It binds the named person to the band and ensures that they are available. Once again it would give you grounds to terminate if you felt that you weren't getting the required amount of work out of them. Management is a 24-hour a day job so it is hard to know how hard they are working, but this clause at least gives the artist a starting point.

*After the end of the Term we shall continue to be entitled to receive our commission at the rates set out below which arise from the exploitation of musical compositions or any of the activities exploited during the Term only.*

- *The rates referred to above are: 15 % in respect of income due in the first five (5) years after the Term.*

Vital clause that states what they can continue to earn, but it must make it clear that this is based on work done during the term *only*. It usually involves past tour income or sponsorship deals they may have previously got you.

*The management shall be responsible for our own general office overhead costs and business expenses (including, without limitation, accountancy fees incurred by us). Any other bona fide expenses reasonably, properly and necessarily incurred solely on your behalf by us in connection with the performance of our obligations hereunder and the enhancement of your career shall be reimbursed by you from monies arising from the Activities.*

Another basic but required clause that tells you what is defined as expenses. This can prove most important when you start to see income generated but can't understand why you are not getting any. The management is entitled to recoup all expenses before accounting their and your slice of income. So keep an eye on all overheads and make sure they are worthwhile.

*You warrant that:*

*you have the right to enter into this Agreement and to grant the rights necessary and shall deliver performances that are artistically consistent with previous performances and are deemed technically and commercially acceptable by the manager in the manager's reasonable opinions and shall be of first class quality. During the Term you will not appoint any third party to act as your manager within the territory in connection with the Activities, nor will you act as your own manager on your own account.*

This is a clause that is usually sped through when reading. However you must adhere to these obligations or you could be putting yourself in potential breach of the contract. This means doing the most important thing an artist can ever do – be a good musician. It sounds obvious, but many of my clients get dragged into free parties and gigs without realising their actual talent is being neglected by themselves! Some clauses will go into more detail about what you can or can't do. As long as they are not too restrictive you must keep to them throughout the contract period.

The biggest problem with management deals is that most obligations on the company will be quite vague, e.g. arranging gigs and promotional events. Many deals may not have some of the clauses above and in my opinion are not real management deals. As well as having these clauses it is favourable to have an appendix to the contract that has a six-month timeframe of plans and events for the band. They don't have to be fixed but show that the company is looking to the future and has real plans for the band. If you do get a deal with no real obligations it may be worth changing it to an agency agreement. This will mean that the company do not have an exclusive right over you which allows you to work with others. Such a decision should not be taken lightly, and it is vital to listen to your legal advice and not allow anyone else to make a decision for you.

The management role can be defined as being responsible for developing and advancing the artist's career. It's the manager's job to liaise with record companies, agents, promoters, lawyers and accountants leaving the artist free to create, perform and record. Essentially the manager focuses on the business side whilst the artist gets on with being creative. So, in keeping with what Rod Smallwood said, the artist needs someone who is efficient, trustworthy, and honest, in keeping the band informed of all business developments through open and clear channels.

# TYPES OF MANAGEMENT

The different types of management are found in the following areas.

## Professional managers

Professional managers make their living solely from artist management and often have one or more clients already working professionally or signed to a major record company. This type of manager usually generates interest from A&R due to their success, and are able to command respect from publishing and record companies. They tend to have wide ranging contacts throughout the music industry and are very well placed.

## Management companies

Comprising groups of managers working together, these are often retained by artists with the personal manager working with the artist on a day-to-day basis. In this case the manager is paid a share of the company's commission. The advantages of being managed by a company with a roster of clients include the opportunity to work with other managed artists, and the knowledge that they will have industry respect and bargaining power. If approached by one of their staff make sure you negotiate an escape route from being managed by the company if your 'key man' decides to leave or is fired.

## Amateur managers

Amateur managers are often referred to as 'baby managers'. This falls into the category of a friend or someone who is still learning the ropes. There are some good music industry-based management courses run at universities that cover all the prerequisites of artist management. These give a solid understanding of what skills a manager needs. With someone starting out, whilst they will have a ton of enthusiasm they will very likely lack the contacts needed or understanding of how to approach labels and organise the general aspects of a band's early career. However, if the young manager is willing and determined to learn then the partnership can be beneficial to both parties.

On a word of caution there are many types of people who profess to be managers, some who have formerly managed one or more successful artists but no longer have clients, or those who are on the periphery of the music business and think they are capable of managing an artist or band. Deal with caution and ensure that you are being represented by someone who is realistic, credible and honest.

## Tour managers

Tour managers are hired by the artist or personal manager to deal with the day-to-day management functions when on the road. This may include getting the band from gig to gig, collecting fees, booking hotels/flights, etc. Unlike a personal manager they are usually paid a straight fee or retainer.

## MANAGEMENT RULES TO REMEMBER

- **Rule 1** Never sign an agreement of any kind with anyone without advice from a qualified music business solicitor.

- **Rule 2** Never use the same solicitor as your manager.

- **Rule 3** *Always* ensure that any contract you sign contains clauses allowing you to walk away from the deal if everything is not to your satisfaction.

- **Rule 4** Agree a contract term of no longer than three years with provisions for termination after 12 months if the management has failed to secure bookings/publishing/record deal or interest in that time.

- **Rule 5** Control the finances yourself. If a manager wishes to open and control a bank account in your name *don't do it*! A reputable manager will be happy to bill you for their commission and expenses, or deduct part or their entire fee from any bookings/deals they secure on your behalf.

● **Rule 6** If you must sign a contract for commission earned on gross income ensure that *all* live work is made an exception. Touring invariably runs at a loss due to the high costs involved!

● **Rule 7** Managers expect the artist to pay for any expenses outside the office, therefore you can expect to be charged for flights/travel, etc on top of the commission fee. If using a manager who has multiple clients ensure any expenses incurred are solely on your behalf, or agree to pay an equal percentage with the other clients.

● **Rule 8** Commissionable income will include income from live gigs, publishing and record advances, royalty and PRS payments, personal/radio and TV appearances, sponsorship, merchandising, etc, and a manager will expect to earn commission on some of these for a period after they no longer manage you.

● **Rule 9** Ensure that you have an independent accountant to check all financial transactions and records on a regular basis.

● **Rule 10** Be careful *not* to agree a verbal contract with anyone, including *enthusiastic mates*, as it could cause problems later on. If someone is helping you out and you don't want him or her to be your manager, tell them and put it in writing.

# Using a Music Agent

During the research for this book it was interesting to note that more and more people were stating that bands should think about getting an agent before they thought about a manager. The reason for this was bands should first build a following before really hitting the record companies, where a manager would then serve their purpose. Let me tell you something, it's just as hard to get an agent as it is anybody else. Agents have the same criteria everyone else looks for, killer bands.

So if you should hear this from anyone, that you should focus on getting an agent, forget it and just focus on what you really need to do. And that is playing live and building your fan-base so that the outside world will come to you.

## WHAT DOES AN AGENT DO?

The agent's role is to book shows for bands. Not just shows, but entire worldwide tours. They will liaise with promoters, negotiate contracts, get the best live fees for you, ensure the running of the gig is like clockwork, along with catering for all a band's needs and wants. They will ensure you get appropriate sound check times, have a rider available, along with meals, transportation and accommodation. They are very professional and will take a ten to 15 per cent from each show you play.

An agent will take all the hard work, stress and hassle of organising gigs and will fight to get you onto some pretty important shows and tours. An agent is worth their weight in gold when the time comes for you to enter the next level of your career. Life on the road is very hectic and to be looked after by a professional will make your life a truckload easier. I know a few agents and have been amazed at how proactive they are in seeking new bands to take on. Most young agents will be out watching gigs every night. They are hungry, motivated and will at some point come across your band. Not having a record deal is no problem for an agent. If they believe you have that special something, they will knock on your door.

Like every other facet of the music industry the days of the dodgy agent are gone. Of course, you may well find low-lifes existing on the fringes but these characters can be seen a mile off. The big guns will have almost every single band currently playing live signed to their roster. If you visit music agent websites you will see which band is signed to whom.

## FROM THE HORSE'S MOUTH

When it came to really finding out more about what an agent does, and more importantly how it will affect an unsigned band, I decided to ask Mark Ngui from Primary Talent and Natasha Bent from The Agency to shed some light.

Mark Ngui: **www.primary.uk.com**

### What is the agent's role in the music industry?

Booking agents are the official representatives of musicians/bands for the purposes of touring. They arrange live performances for their artists. You can have more than one booking agent. Normally this would be split as one agent for the world excluding North America and one for North America.

### What does it mean for a band when they sign to an agent?

If an agent does work with you, along with the commission you'll be paying them, you hope they could in turn increase your fee, and help (working alongside your manager) to get you opening slots for larger bands, festivals, etc.

### Should bands approach agents or do agents prefer to find bands?

Personal preference. Any artist should really wait until they are approached for all areas of management, PR, agency, etc – it would mean they are getting something right! I personally have only ever taken on a band whose management has approached me once. Not to say that I won't listen to unsolicited demos, but it is very rare that an artist will join my roster from having approached me through sending an unsolicited demo or cold email.

### Does a band need a record deal to sign to an agent?

There are so many bands out there, and because agents know the market will only support so many shows, they have to be picky to serve their clients well. So, usually, they take bands that have a record label that will help promote the shows, since, if they sell too many bad shows, they'll end up just like the unknown band calling their local venue: no one will call them back.

### How long does an agent deal last for?

There is no term. Working with an agent in the UK, the artist will have to agree in writing to standard terms and conditions of business (required by UK agency law). But normally there is no other contract between the artist and agent that binds them to work together over a set amount of time.

### What does an agent look for in a band?

There are many different criteria that an agent might look for in a band. Above all, do they believe in the band, whether they think the band are going to be 'successful' (taken to mean whatever you/they may deem as successful).

### How does the agent/band relationship work?

The agent will 99 per cent of the time work with the Artist's manager. The agent will work with their manager and liaise with their label(s) (product manager(s)).

## Natasha Bent: **www.theagencygroup.com**

### What is the agent's role in the music industry?

I would say that the agent's basic role is to look after the live side of a band's/musician's career (worldwide, or whichever territories you agree to cover with management). To work closely with the management and band first, and the team around the band (label, press, radio, online marketing, regional, national...) to give advice on the live side, so that we can all work towards achieving the same goals.

### What does it mean for a band when they sign to an agent?

When a band decides to go with an agent, basically the agent takes on the role (as mentioned above). There are no contracts between bands and agents, so a good relationship is vital. The agent has to then look after the band's live side (gigs, tours, festivals) in decided territories. The band can only have one agent for each territory.

As a general rule, I would be the agent worldwide excluding North America. The band would then have an agent for North America and may also decide to work with a Canadian agent. On average, an agent would take ten per cent commission from every live show/event they book.

### Should bands approach agents or do agents prefer to find bands?

It depends on the stage the band is at. There are so many bands presently that it's difficult, as there aren't enough agents in ratio to the number of bands there are. If you are a band that has great/reputable management and possibly already a label deal, then as agents we would be aware of this, and we would go to the bands. It's not uncommon for more then one agent to be going for a band. However, at early stages this may not be the case. It's good for a band to create their own hype (even if it's local to their area) and then start approaching agents. But I would advise that the band should research agents and agencies first, to make sure they are targeting the right person/people.

### Does a band need a record deal to sign to an agent?

It also depends on the agent. I currently have three bands on my roster that aren't signed, but I enjoy working with bands from an early stage. As an agent, I personally work with bands that I will believe will be signed and have success in the long term. Again, it depends on the agent. I have only been an agent for three years, and love working with new acts, building them from scratch, but this may differ with each agent.

### How long does an agent deal last for?

As there are no contracts, an agent can work with a band for as short or as long as the relationship is good between the agent and management/band. The agent can decide to stop working with a band, but equally, the same can happen the other way around.

### What does an agent look for in a band?

I think this is a difficult question and will certainly differ for each agent. Personally, I look firstly for a great unique style to each band I work with. I make sure that I don't have two of the same sounding bands (so that I am not making my acts compete for opportunities that I am going for). It definitely helps for the band to have management (that have a good music business knowledge) and backing does help (A&R interest at least). I look to see if bands have done a lot of the ground work, and created their own hype (local press/local fanbase/MySpace/own promotions) as that to me is a great quality to have.

### How does the agent/band relationship work?

An agent basically works for the band/management so we can give our advice, but ultimately the decisions lie with management/band. We have to make sure that our bookings coincide with the label's plans.

### How did you become involved in being a music agent?

After university I decided to go to music college to study singing for a year (as this was always a passion since I was young). During this course we had business lessons once a week where key industry reps would come in to talk about their side of the business. The more I learnt about the business, the less I wanted to make money out of my music. I did backing singing for Carleen Anderson for a year, which was a great experience, but again, I wanted to keep my singing as enjoyment.

So in business lessons I would stay behind and speak to all the key industry reps to get advice, and with some, work experience. I (like many in music) started from scratch, and worked for free for various labels/press people for six months (still not knowing which area I wanted to go into). I then got my first job as a manager's assistant (First Column Management, Brighton) and gained fantastic experience and knowledge from Phil Nelson. He then suggested that I would make a good agent and introduced me to Charlie Myatt, who runs 13Artists. And from then on, I absolutely loved it. As I love music so much, I get to be at shows a lot and this job allows me to travel the world. My family are international, and so this job really suits me. There is nothing more amazing than watching a band go from playing to five people a show, to selling out their first London Astoria gig!

One thing I would say, being a fellow musician also, is that a band needs to remember that it is a *business* they are entering, and it's difficult. You need to be thick skinned, take criticism (as long as it's constructive) and be able to be away from home/family for long periods of time. You need to have people around you that you can trust and great belief in your abilities.

## FROM ZERO TO HERO

And there you are. Always better to get information straight from the source. You now have an insight to what agents do and think. If your live performance is doing the business and you're pulling in crowds the news will get back to an agent who will then blaze a trail to your next gig. And it's very possible you will go from zero to hero very quickly indeed!

# Working with Promoters

Promoters exist to promote live shows.

## WHAT PROMOTERS DO

Promoters organise the shows as well as liaising with music agents to book bands. They will secure the venues for a show and take care of the promotional activity surrounding the gigs via the media. This will include national press campaigns, internet activity, regional and local activity, and will work directly with music agents and bands to cover everything the bands need to play. If it's a huge headlining band then the stage set may well be planned around their needs, taking care of the lighting rig and PA system.

The promoter pays the band, but obviously not all bands will get the same deals. Promoters will work with agents and managers to secure the best deal for the bands. Headline bands may get upwards to a million, whilst smaller bands get the exposure and perhaps expenses. This is at the top level with promoters such as Livenation who take care of events like Download and Reading, etc.

## A PROMOTER EXPLAINS HIS ROLE

I sat down with Jon Dunn to get an insight into what he looks for in bands and how he came to get involved in promoting.

*Can you define what a promoter's role is?*

I think my role is to find the best new talent out there. And then to define with the band where they want to go, not just musically but creatively, whether they want to play big venues or small ones. Some acts may not want to be big. Some acts are very artistic and are happy to keep things on a smaller scale. So first and foremost I get an idea of where the band needs to go. And then from there it's a case of knowing what's missing from the band. Are they missing a manager, an A&R man, a record deal, a publishing deal? Perhaps some press is needed. I tend to get involved in that early and try to help find the missing pieces from the band's armoury.

I then tend to gauge how fast they want this to happen. Again some bands tend to be at a stage where they are not ready to play six songs, they may have only two great tracks. I think they need a critical eye to understand when they are ready to play in front of A&R, or the industry or reviewers, because if all that is done at the wrong time it can hamper the band.

So, first and foremost is to get a solid foundation, and how I would do that would be through contacts in the industry, send it on to other people, build a team around the band and just nurture it from there. Then to develop them further get them playing in front of pub audiences in out of town shows away from their fan base in front of a neutral audience. If you get them to develop that way you tend to see their confidence grow and there may come a point where they have their best songs, some great performances and a good team developing around them.

That for me is when we really start, start to look for some really good support slots. I make sure any time they do their own headline shows we get the press involved, and we start synchronising events so it all happens at the right time. I generally like to mix it up and do one or two headliners in a strong town and perhaps a little one in London along with some support slots. And all of this is about developing them as a live band and maximising their ticket sales at that point as well.

I personally thought this was one of the most considered and thoughtful answers I was given from any interview conducted for this book. It gives a great insight into how promoters think or perhaps should think.

My next question to Jon is for all of you who would like to get into the promoting side of the music business.

### So Jon, how did you get involved in promoting?

I was in a band and I was singing. We were a spoof band and I was particularly rubbish, trying to be funny, but ultimately I realised the joke was probably on me, and although we could get 200 people in our home town if I went ten miles up the road I didn't know anyone and no one would come and see us. I soon realised we were talentless, and thought the best way to have lots of friends and maybe meet some girls and maximise my ego was to put on some shows. And to be honest I started off with some local gigs and it took off from there. That was in Chelmsford at the Y Club and then I moved to the Colchester Arts Centre. The Arts Centre taught me to think outside of just booking gigs. I started to book jazz and world music. It teaches you how to develop your skills in where to find an audience. It's very easy to just place an advert in *NME* because that's where your audience is. With world and jazz you have to think a lot more creatively in finding that audience.

I then went to Northampton and worked at the Roadmenders which led me to develop my own company for about three years. We used to do small shows across 15 towns. From there I went to the Mackenzie group booking in Islington, Shepherd's Bush, Brixton, Liverpool, Glasgow, Birmingham and Bristol Academies, which again led me onto Livenation where I've been for about two years.

As for anyone trying to break into being a promoter I'm sad to say it's tougher now, much tougher than when I got started. Back then as a promoter you could put a band on, give them some beers, give them some food, pay the band and generally run a show. Now for a small promoter in a small venue it's much tougher. There's finance to contribute to national ads, there's VAT on top of that which they can't claim back if they are not registered, the riders have got bigger, there is always a tour support now where there never used to be. There would be the local bands you could put on to bring some people in. It's just become a much tougher environment due to the industry becoming that much more professional.

I would suggest that a young promoter doesn't stretch himself, one show a week is a good start, or even one show every two weeks, by setting up a club with good bands and creating that club environment. There are a lot of clubs coming out now, especially further up north, with art rock style clubs developing good local scenes for the kids to get into. It is easier to promote one genre of music initially than it is trying to be an all rounder. But it's a good and essential starting point to get well versed in one musical area.

### What possibility is there for unsigned bands getting a chance to play a major festival?

Personally I would give unsigned bands a chance to play a major festival. If I liked them that much they would get a chance. I'd hate to think I could never put on a band because they haven't got an agent or a record deal, that would be the end for me. I really think there has to be a freedom to be able to put something on if you believe in it. It has to fit with the festival. As an example, across all the festivals this year there are around 80 bands that won't have agents, but will have a bit of a story to them or some really good ideas. They may be getting really good press or a good reaction from the kids, or it could be the labels or agents haven't got onto to it yet. And in many ways this can actually drive interest from the industry to take that band onto the next level of their careers.

But it's not just about exposure for the band, it's actually about perception. If it can break a band by being on the bottom of a full page advert for the festival, and someone saying I don't know this band but I know the rest of the bill so I'll check that band out, then that's all the better. For me I will hopefully be remembered for doing that. If I believe in a band and they are really talented then I want to help push them along.

This was a worthwhile interview for me because someone as experienced and talented as Jon gives some good insights into how promoters think and work. Most bands, however, will be at the start of their careers, so I asked Nicholas Barnet from Dead or Alive promotions, based in London, how bands should approach promoters.

### Nicholas, what should bands be doing at this level?

Bands need to be at least semi-professional in how they conduct themselves. Promoters don't expect bands at this level to run themselves like a business, but a level of professionalism is required. This helps the gig run smoothly and ensures where possible a stress-free evening and makes everybody happy. This includes bands turning up to sound check on time, communication with the other bands playing the same bill on sharing the drum kit, or amps, and making a plan to ensure where possible no misunderstandings. Little things like this don't take much effort and do make the night a lot more stress-free. Younger bands, or bands with no real gigging experience, are not organised and have an attitude that rubs promoters up the wrong way. If the promoter is stressed or unhappy that can pass on to the bands. Some promoters deal with 20 odd bands per week and you can often tell straightaway which level the bands are at. It's not so much the hassle but the attitude of some bands. If it goes wrong because of an attitude the band often wonder why they don't get asked back for another gig. So they really shoot themselves in the feet.

This is where an experienced manager comes in handy, they can steer them through these learning curves. A manager should be the one most responsible and best organised to deal with the rest of the acts on the bill. If you don't have a manager at this stage then it's worth picking the best communicator in the band to organise the logistics. It doesn't really take bands that long to get experienced and if they wish to have a career out of it they should learn quickly.

### So how do bands go about booking gigs?

Simply by emailing me or sending me a CD. But I tend to really only book London-based bands although if I hear something in the music then I will give it a chance. I tend to hear music from all over the UK and lately from around the world. An example of the reason I'm mostly only booking London-based bands is I had a band from Italy headline a show who assured me of a good sized fan base, but the reality was that no one showed up. And unfortunately that's the same if the band are from Manchester or Leeds, etc. You can't expect a bus load of kids to come down to see their band in London. I will put on bands who I think are interesting and take a chance, but most bands are not able to pull a crowd. And this isn't limited to London, it happens locally too. Most local venues have the same policy about putting on out of town bands who aren't proven. And whilst promoters start off with good intentions the financial reality bites and you are faced with being chucked out of your venue.

Regional promoters are faced with the same realities, which is why you tend to see the same bands playing the same venues until one of those bands breaks through. It's just an unfair scenario for bands asking their mates to travel to other towns to support them as this costs a lot of money. Time off work, and flying up and down motorways on a regular basis is just not tenable when they can just pop along to the local venue for a good night out. Some bands can do this, and without the support of a promoter who needs them to sell a certain amount of tickets beforehand, but I think this puts undue pressure on a band. It's not necessary either because there's this big myth that you have to play in London to get spotted. This debate goes on *ad infinitum*, but you are just as likely to get spotted playing your home town as anywhere else. The A&R in this country prefer to get out of town as they know there is a better chance to see great bands. Obviously there are some A&R who won't get out of zone 2 but a lot would go to the most obscure places to see genius bands. Some bands want to play London but they do it for the wrong reasons. You are not really likely to get any A&R presence down here.

### Finally, Nicholas, what advice would you give to unsigned bands?

Concentrate on the demo. Get the best recording you can and do the best job you can with the songs. Recording is more like a science than an art and whilst home recording studios have freed bands to record at their leisure many find it hard to utilise the equipment. It's worth getting a professional job first, which will cost money, but it's not worth sending out badly recorded CDs in this day and age. So bands should consider getting an engineer or a producer involved until they understand the basics of recording music. As an example I'm working with two bands at the moment, one wouldn't know how to turn a computer on but the other have developed a totally professional CD using equipment at home. Whichever way bands record, they have to make sure it is on a par with the rest otherwise the CD won't get in through the door.

## LOOKING AT A CONTRACT

Sound advice from both ends of the promoter spectrum I think. Approaching a promoter with an email or CD is the first part of booking a live gig. You may be lucky enough and have a promoter approach you. However if you don't, when you send in a CD make sure you have the accompanying letter with who you are and where you come from. Never expect a promoter to know who you are. So make sure you have a contact number, website and email address on the CD in case it ever gets separated from the press pack. Below is a sample contract that many promoters will send to you. Again, this is just for educational purposes but it gives you an idea of what to expect.

### Promoter agreement

Please could you read this agreement and reply by sending it back via email with your details typed in at the bottom of the page.

NB1 By law, the venue cannot allow anyone inside under 18 years of age. If anyone in the band is under 18 please contact (promoters) immediately. It is strongly recommended that bands advise fans who are recently 18+ (or who look young!) to carry ID with them as if it is not produced on demand entry to the venue will be denied. (The Town) *council is really applying pressure on the venue about this, I'm afraid, so it is strictly enforced.*

NB2 If you haven't sent press details, reviews, juicy quotes, or website addresses to me already then please do so as these will go out in the listings and mailouts.

NB3 Please could you bill the show as (the promoter presents).

*Agreement*

The Promoter Presents

Wednesday 25 December 2007

8pm – 11pm

The Dog and Bucket pub, 7 Banana Street, Neverland SW1 (Piccadilly Circus/Leicester Sq). (Tubes: Piccadilly Circus/Leicester Sq.)

*Performances/soundcheck times/contact details*

Band number 1: 10.30 – 11.00pm/sc: 5.30 – 6.00pm

Band number 2: 9.45 – 10.15pm/sc: 6.00 – 6.30pm

Band number 3: 9.00 – 9.30pm/sc: 6.30 – 7.00pm

Band number 4: 8.15 – 8.45pm/sc: 7.00 – 7.30pm

Important message: the venue has a very strict 11pm curfew. Gigs have been over-running and this is actually illegal and could result in members of staff losing their jobs and it being impossible to promote any more shows at this venue. To prevent this from happening (the promoter) is now insisting that bands keep to their alloted set times. Rather than penalise the last band by cutting them short, no band will be allowed to overrun their allotted set time and will be cut off if they do so. As such, please ensure that you start your set on time and keep it to 30 minutes.

Load-in from 5.30pm. The bands must be present for the sound check at the time given or they may not receive a sound check.

Please remember about congestion charges: cost £8/penalty £40 – £120!

Payment from Post Offices/self-service machines/petrol stations/phone: 0845 900 1234 or you can pay at some tube stations: www.cclondon.com

*Door prices*

The door charge is £4 with flyer or concessions. £5 without.

*!!!!! Drinks special !!!!!*

There are always drink promotions available at the venue. Please check on the night at the venue what these are. A typical example is: £5 for the following: 2 x cocktails; 3 x shooters; 6 x shots of schnapps; 2 x large glasses and the rest of the bottle *free* on selected wines.

*Rebooking policy*

15+ people = a re-booking.

30+ people = a booking at (a bigger venue).

Any damages to equipment provided by either the PA suppliers (the promoter) must be paid for.

Also, please do not place posters (without prior permission) or any stickers in the venue at all, otherwise the management will charge for damages.

*Flyposting*

Please do not flypost gigs. This now leads to very heavy prosecution by the local council authorities for both the venue and the bands!

(the promoter) and (the venue) cannot accept any liability for lost equipment or personal belongings of the bands.

Please complete:

Name....................................................................

On behalf of the

band....................................................................

Position: e.g. Bandmember

Manager................................................................

Many thanks

The promoter

# Societies to Support Musicians

Whilst doing the research for this subject I was concerned with the lack of understanding shown by bands when it came to the MCPS (Mechanical Copyright Protection Society) and the PRS (Performing Right Society). The main question of many music websites was 'Is it worth it to join PRS?' A very valid question in my book; but what surprised me were the responses from many of our so-called internet experts who said that for many bands it wasn't really relevant. Well, I'm here to tell you that being a member of MCPS-PRS is very relevant and very beneficial. The point of this whole book is to give bands the understanding that they can make money from a career in music, but need to consider all areas and potential income streams. You will never have enough time in the day to cover every aspect of your career from an administration point of view, so being a member of any organisation that exists to collect royalties is a definite must.

I've taken all the information you need to understand about MCPS-PRS directly from the website to give you a full and thorough understanding of what this society does. Also, just before the MCPS section there is a Q&A interview I had with Myles Keller who is the MCPS-PRS Membership Development Director to give you a more personal insight. It makes good reading.

## THE PERFORMING RIGHT SOCIETY

### What is PRS?

Established in 1914, the Performing Right Society (PRS) is a non-profit-making membership organisation of composers, songwriters, authors and publishers of music of all styles including classical, pop, jazz and music for films, adverts and TV. The essential function of PRS is to collect and distribute music royalties on behalf of its members.

## What does PRS do?

PRS is known as a 'collecting society' because its primary role is collecting royalties from music users in the UK who every day publicly perform, broadcast and include music in cable production services. PRS also collects royalties from around the world for its members through reciprocal agreements with collecting societies overseas.

PRS collects the royalties by issuing a licence to the music user (usually charged on an annual basis). In order to then make royalty payments to its members, PRS needs to know what music is being played. Major users, such as the BBC and large concert venues, give PRS detailed reports of the music they play. For many other venues including commercial discos, clubs and pubs, PRS sends researchers to obtain first-hand information.

With an estimated 8 billion public performances in the UK every year it is not possible to track every one. To pay out these royalties, statistical methods are used based on actual performance information. After recovering its minimal running costs PRS pays all the remaining money collected to its UK and overseas members.

## What are the criteria to join?

Writers: This category includes composers, lyric authors, songwriters and arrangers. All must have a work that has been broadcast, performed live or played in public.

Publishers: Publishers must have contracts covering at least 15 works.

Successors: If you would like to find out more about how successor members are admitted, please contact Member Admissions at **www.mcps-prs-alliance.co.uk**

## What proof is required?

Writers and publishers: will be required to provide a letter from a broadcaster, promoter or venue owner confirming the broadcast or performance.

Successors: would normally be appointed in a will, so PRS always tries to act so that the royalties can be paid as set out in the will or by the law.

## What is the joining fee?

Writers: pay a one-off fee of £100 (including VAT).

Publishers: pay a one-off fee of £400 (including VAT).

Successors: to deceased members are *not* required to pay a fee.

There is no annual membership fee.

**Does my music have to have been published to become a PRS member?**

No, it does not.

**Do I automatically become a member of MCPS as well?**

No. The Mechanical-Copyright Protection Society is a separate organisation in terms of membership and the rights it licenses. PRS and MCPS have formed an operational alliance which provides administrative services to both societies, but membership of one does not constitute membership of the other.

So that's the information you need about PRS. Before we hit MCPS I raised ten questions with membership director Myles Keller on the benefits to unsigned bands of joining PRS.

**Once a band signs up to PRS, how does it work for them?**

Ultimately you as a writer or composer will assign your copyrights to us for the world. We will collect your royalties for all of your 'works' (songs, compositions, jingles – whatever you write musically) in the UK and from the other societies around the world. We send you quarterly 'distributions' which are payments and statements for all of your income from live work, radio or television broadcasts, internet and mobile income and your international royalties – unlike almost every other society in the world.

**Are unsigned bands important to PRS?**

Unsigned or not, the whole supposition for membership qualification is that you should have a 'work' either broadcast or performed publicly (gigs are fine). If you are unsigned, that is not a bad thing, you just need your music 'out there'.

**How would a band make money membership of the PRS, on an unsigned level, and whilst playing gigs?**

We have something called the gigs and clubs scheme. Basically, you let us know when and where you've been playing. Music researchers are sent to collect performance details direct from performers at statistically valid random samples of venues across the UK. Members playing in venues of this size should consider participating in the PRS Gigs and Clubs Scheme, though conditions do apply.

**Is it true that the more gigs you play, the more money you can make?**

The more gigs you play – and you must ensure we are notified by sending us in your set lists signed by promoters and dated – could earn you thousands of pounds over time.

### Are all unsigned (PRS members) bands entitled to a share of the monies collected?

No, you must be a PRS member to receive any PRS income with your name on it. You have to be in it to win it.

### Does this make the band more professional?

I think membership of PRS and PPL, for example, just indicate that an artist is savvy and aware that record sales and concert tickets are not the only way to earn money from your craft, in fact, increasingly we are seeing that PRS income is by far the greatest source of income. Writers of all music have to start really opening their eyes to the 'business' that they are in.

### Does being a member of PRS give unsigned artists support in a professional sense?

We have a number of schemes and ways of supporting our members. We have the PRS Foundation For New Music which is the UK's largest independent funder for new music, and we have the PRS Members' Fund, which is a registered charity formed to help members and their dependants who are in need of financial support. We are frequently becoming more active in showcasing and supporting our members who play live. There is a PRS loan scheme, limited, but useful to anyone who may require some upfront money. We also have a legal and accountancy referral scheme.

### Is it down to the band to submit their set lists or down to the promoter?

It's down to the promoter at a certain level and beyond, say from the barfly up, but I would *always* back up what other people say they are going to do and submit my own set lists, religiously. The set list forms can be downloaded from the MCPS-PRS website so there is no excuse if you've left them behind or a promoter says they haven't got any forms available on the night.

### Should all bands consider joining PRS?

Yes, every writer, every composer who has a song or work that is aired on radio, TV, on the internet, or played live should join. The £100 joining fee may be the only guarantee of seeing a financial return from this increasingly difficult business.

### And what advantage does PRS have over its American counterparts?

We collect for you in the UK and pay you quarterly for *every* income stream. This is unprecedented. We pay more money, more quickly and take fewer deductions from our members than our American counterparts. We also have a scheme called the Live Concert Service for our bigger touring writers, which is something for discussing at a major touring level.

Overall I think a very cool insight for anyone looking to join PRS. We now look at what MCPS does.

# THE MECHANICAL COPYRIGHT PROTECTION SOCIETY

## About the MCPS

The Mechanical Copyright Protection Society (MCPS), established in 1924, is a not-for-profit organisation which currently represents over 18,000 composers, songwriters and music publishers.

The essential function of MCPS is to collect and distribute royalties. It acts on behalf of its members by negotiating agreements with those who wish to record and distribute product containing copyright musical works and collecting licence fees for this use. The money is subsequently distributed to its members as mechanical royalties.

## What MCPS does

MCPS is known as a collecting society because its main role is collecting money from music users in the UK who record music into TV and radio programmes, websites, feature films, CDs, records and so on. MCPS collects royalties by issuing licences to music users in respect of the mechanical copyright in musical works.

Details of the music used are supplied to MCPS by the licensees. This information, when matched to the detailed work information held on the MCPS databases, enables the payment of royalties to the writers and publishers of the music used.

MCPS is funded by the commission it levies on the licence revenue it receives.

## What Mechanical Right means

The Copyright Designs & Patents Act 1988 gives a copyright owner control of five restricted acts in relation to his/her copyright musical work.

The 'mechanical right', as administered by MCPS, consists of two of these rights:

● the right to copy the work

● the right to issue copies of the work in public.

This means that every time a work is copied, or a copy is issued to the public, royalties generated from its licensing will be collected by MCPS and paid on to its members.

MCPS publishes a useful leaflet, *What is MCPS?* which includes all of the above information and more. Click here for a download-able version on their website (see end of chapter), or email communication@mcps-prs-alliance.co.uk if you wish to receive one or more printed copies of the leaflet. Please note that there will be a charge for postage on large quantities.

## A brief history of MCPS

The Mechanical Copyright Licences Company Ltd (MECOLICO) was established in 1910 in anticipation of the Copyright Act 1911. Its purpose was to collect and distribute mechanical royalties due from the new gramophone companies.

Shortly afterwards the Copyright Protection Society Ltd was founded and, in 1924, a merger of the two bodies resulted in the Mechanical-Copyright Protection Society Limited (MCPS).

MCPS has been wholly owned by the Music Publishers' Association (MPA) since 1976.

# BENEFITS OF MCPS MEMBERSHIP

## Who can become a member of MCPS

Writers and publishers of music are eligible for membership if their music has been copied, or is due to be copied, onto one or more of the many sound-carrying formats, including but not limited to:

- CDs
- records
- audio tapes
- music DVDs
- TV and radio
- videos
- computer games
- feature films
- websites
- telephone ringtones
- novelty products
- commercials.

Writers who have assigned their works to a music publisher do not generally need to join MCPS as the publisher will collect the mechanical royalties and pass the writer share on to them.

## The benefits

- **Maximising revenue** As the representative body of over 16,000 members, MCPS works to maximise the rates levied for use of its members' works and to protect its members' rights.

- **Influence** Through its operational alliance with the Performing Right Society, MCPS is one of the biggest and most influential collection societies in the world, representing its members not only nationally but also throughout the international community.

- **Rights** In conjunction with other leading industry organisations such as British Music Rights, MCPS has developed an effective lobbying position nationally and internationally, with the aim of protecting members' interests and influencing new legislation in favour of rights holders.

- **Anti-piracy** Along with enforcement agencies, MCPS runs a UK-wide anti-piracy programme to crack down on counterfeits and illegal copying of members' music.

- **Protection** MCPS plays a crucial wider industry role in rights protection through licence scheme negotiation and Copyright Tribunal defences to maintain the value of the rights administered.

- **Transparency** MCPS treats all members equally and operates one of the most transparent operations of any collection society in the world.

- **Efficiency** MCPS offers superb administrative efficiency and accuracy in licensing through its thorough knowledge of music users and the music industry in general.

- **Usage** MCPS offers schemes for all types of usage of its members' works within the physical, mobile and online world, including a joint MCPS-PRS online licensing model for music downloads.

MCPS takes a proactive approach in the development of its existing licensing schemes to adapt to changing uses of music, and is constantly developing new schemes to deal with new technologies.

- **Royalties** MCPS delivers millions of itemised lines of royalty income to its members every year via high volume transaction processing. It offers a very high percentage of full census distributions, ensuring that royalties are distributed to the copyright owners of actual works used. MCPS regularly monitors and audits music users to ensure compliance, and operates an efficient credit management system to ensure all royalties due are paid in full to its members. MCPS distributes royalties to its members monthly and provides distribution statements containing accurate accounting on a work by work basis of the exact usage. Member statements can be provided in different formats including via email and online (through secure FTP).

MCPS operates a highly efficient backclaims procedure allowing the payment to its members of all pipeline royalties.

- **Value** MCPS has no annual membership fee and operates with an average commission rate of 6.4 per cent (2003), representing good value for money for members.

- **Choice** Members can choose to license direct (for example films or ads) or else leave the negotiation and processing to MCPS.

- **Services** MCPS canvasses opinions from and reacts purposefully to its members' proposals for strengthening the protection of their rights and increasing the value of their copyrights. MCPS provides fast, efficient and friendly member services, offering a single point of contact for all types of member enquiry with highly trained staff ready and waiting to help. MCPS facilitates the ongoing licensing and collection of royalties while members resolve duplicate claims and sample clearances.

## Other benefits

MCPS provides free online access to a range of services and information including works/productions/statements and unmatched files.

It distributes a free magazine four times a year to all members, which provides information, business news and interesting features. It also distributes a free monthly e-mail bulletin with up-to-date business news.

## Joining fee

There is a one-off administration charge of £50 per member per application. The same rate applies for writers as for publishers.

## TAKE THE NEXT STEP

Right then, you now have all the info and data to understand what these societies do and how beneficial they are to your career. It's down to you to implement what you now know. Here's how to contact the societies:

www.mcps-prs-alliance.co.uk

www.prsfoundation.co.uk

www.prsmembersfund.co.uk

# Being in a Band

*ii*

**Music is thy one true God**

Commandment Two

Give me a thousand kids with a thousand guitars over a thousand kids with a thousand guns every time. Instead of governments recruiting people to join armies that kill, maim and destroy in the name of liberty and freedom, they should recruit people to form bands, make music, play gigs and give the people the time of their lives. But they don't. There is more money to be made in killing with hatred than inspiring with love.

## CHANGING LIVES

So my friends it's your job to become the revolutionary in its truest sense. To educate with lyrics, to create mini sonic tapestries, to make people feel the hairs on the back of their necks stand up when the piece of music that you have written does its job. Music has the power to bring the world together. And perhaps (it kills me to say it) a band may never change how the world works, but music in all its forms has the power to change people's lives.

Music has the power to heal. Music is the one true universal language and it has done far more good for the soul than anything that has ever been expressed though the mouth of a politician. Why do you think the establishment has been so anti-rock and roll? Why has music been banned from countries with dictators for so long and why, even, did the Tony Blair government court the rock and roll stars of the 1990s? Because it's the one true thing left that will always be cool. It's the one medium that can bring revolution to people's lives. It can make the greatest difference. Be it a protest song or a love song, at some point in your life a song you heard changed the way you thought and lived from that day forth. And in doing so made you want to pick up a guitar and join a band. This is why you are here.

## Music as revolution

The introduction to this chapter was intended to be dramatic. It's a call to arms, a war cry and a revolutionary flag in the sand expressing enough is enough. You cannot look at the world today without asking why things are so wrong. The politicians are taking us to the brink. The people are too busy with their lives to think. And so my friends, as musical revolutionaries it is your job to wake us all up. Music is the one thing we have left to help change the world. So don't be demure in stepping up.

> We are the music makers. We are the dreamers of dreams…

What was that quote from Charlie and the Chocolate Factory? *We are the music makers. We are the dreamers of dreams…*

Despite the manufactured bullshit of *X Factor*, *Pop Idol* and most of the top 40, music is still a platform for true self-expression. Music retains a power that comes direct from the soul. Without deceit, manipulation or lies, when you listen to a great song, a lovely piece of music, it comes from a place where only angels tread. And that's why in this day and age we need bands more than we ever did. We need more kids picking up the guitar, to sing, to rebel and to heal us all. A great song is for all time.

## WHY FORM A BAND?

Being involved with music is a life-long journey. Forming a band and keeping it running is no easy task. You will be hungry, broke and fantastically out of sync with the rest of humanity. As AC/DC once said, *It's a long way to the top if you wanna rock and roll.* No truer words were ever spoken. Your fuel for the long ride is passion. If you are passionate then you need to remain passionate through the entire ride. Yes, it's a business too but your passion must remain undiminished. Life in music is a roller coaster ride of extreme highs and lows. Everyone will throw their opinions at

> It's a long way to the top if you wanna rock and roll.

you. What you should do, what you shouldn't do (music experts), that you should get a job (family, friends, etc). Uncle Freddie has an opening down at the factory…

Unless they invest the same blood and sweat as you, or are willing to go hungry when you go hungry, or put their money where their mouth is and despite what you read or are told by the experts, if it doesn't feel right in your guts don't do it. You will have no way of knowing what kind of success awaits you if any at all. Write your dreams and plans down. Make a plan of what you want to achieve with timelines and stick to them. Define success on your own terms. If you don't know what you want to achieve it will never come to you. And whilst bands come and go the music remains alive.

## EVOLUTION OF A BAND

A band is essentially a gang. Being in a band should be tribal. It is after all you against the world. But, any chain is only ever as strong as its weakest link. And for most bands who start out as friends the transition process from being mates into a professional outfit can be very hurtful and destroy friendships. When exposed to the music industry the first question many managers or A&R will ask themselves is if there are any band members who do not cut it. This is a reality and a very harsh one to face for young bands with dreams. But the question is a valid one. Having a guitar player not up to scratch, or a drummer who can't keep time will hold a band back. Likewise, having a singer with no charisma or stage presence will do no favours for you. And as a band you should right from the start, if you are seriously intent on getting somewhere, ask yourselves if you have a band member who is holding you back. Most bands do not remain unscathed from this process and if it benefits them all when changes are made for the good of the band then that's the natural law of progress, however harsh it may seem.

Finding the right member for any band is a massive undertaking. This is down to you and if you are unsigned you are always limited to the town you hale from in choosing the right band members. Is it better to form the band and get out there, yes always, but I'm just making the point that at some point this issue will arise and you will have to face it. The point of this book is not to tell you how to put your band together, it's to give you an understanding of the issues you will at some time have to reluctantly embrace.

## Advertising for band members

In this digital age there is no excuse for not advertising for potential members. The days are gone where you stuck a scruffy piece of paper on the local music shop noticeboard looking for the next hit shot guitarist. Now you have access to unlimited websites that cover every musical angle you can think of. Each town has a local music forum. Most towns have a college or university. You have access to a pool of people that play instruments and who are looking to join a band. Advertise everywhere and make the adverts as cool as you can.

## Creating the band's nucleus

The point here is to simply form the nucleus of the band. Diamonds aren't mined from the caves of doom bright, sparkly and ready to hit the shops. And neither are bands. You will go through a process of intense pressure and development before you are ready to storm the world. The good news is that it is a lot of fun. The not so good news is that it's slightly harder work than you will expect. The even better news is that you will have the time of your life.

## THE BAND AS A BUSINESS

When a band is young all they have are songs and dreams. No money is being made. Everyone is broke and the business aspect of it never comes to mind, partly because it's so far away and partly because some bands will never get to that stage. But it's worth considering from the start that a band is a business and the more you are prepared the more ready you are for any prosepective ambushes further down the road. I've seen bands live as collectives.

They all live together, pool their money, cover all the band's needs and share everything evenly. At the start this is a good idea but the circumstances never last long. They simply cannot.

When it comes to business its worth knowing who is entitled to what share the band makes depending on who puts the most in, e.g. songwriting publishing. The songwriter gets the most because they write the songs. And it is always a shock to the other members when the money comes in and all of a sudden the drunken nights dreaming of being rich evaporate due to the songwriter getting the lion's share of the cake. Of course the shock does come much sooner than I'm suggesting. It's when the publishing contract is signed that the band members really find out who is on what percentage. Always, it's down to the songwriters to decide who gets a percentage of the publishing. But learning about these things now will save upset later on and we will deal with band agreements shortly.

## The hierarchy

A band is not a democracy, nor will it ever be. There is almost always one creative force, or perhaps two, in every band. This is the songwriting force. They are the ones with the vision and whilst you may lend to the band with your style of drumming or guitar sound, without the songs you are just another member of the band. It can be argued with merit that the vocals are the most important aspect of a band and whilst it remains that some bands never recover when their singer does a solo job, a lot of big bands do carry on. Not really the case in today's music industry due to bands disappearing very quickly, but certainly older bands like Genesis, Marillion, AC/DC *et al.* But to be honest those bands were of a generation with fans that grew up with their bands. If Oasis or Radiohead lost their singers it would be the end of them.

So, put aside the dreams for a minute and let's get the frustrating business side out in the open so you are all aware of what needs to be understood. Most bands understand there is a hierarchy anyway, but let's shine light on those dark places shall we?

## BAND AGREEMENTS

Band agreements really come into force once you have signed a record deal with the prospect of making money. It is always good to have them signed before any deals come along for the band's peace of mind, as well as projecting a more professional image to potential suitors. The band must sit down and discuss the various issues relating to setting the band up as a business. And whilst some artists never set up band agreements it's a good idea to read the basics a band agreement should cover.

Just like any other contract the band agreement is a set of rules or conditions that each member agrees to stick to that relates to all band activities such as ownership of name and songwriting splits. It can be drafted as a partnership agreement, which means it carries a bit more legal weight and is governed by the appropriate statute. This should be discussed as soon as possible, even if the band has just formed and it should cover some or all of the following main terms.

- **Musical credit** This should come at the beginning of the contract, stating the various definitions of compositions, contributions and credits.

- **Copyright** Deals with the various rights in the music, defining and setting out the meanings.

- **Song ownership** Can set out all the song splits plus any third party interests, so if someone outside the band has contributed to a song then it becomes the band's responsibility to account for and protect their interest.

- **Income distribution** Defines the possible income streams from digital to tour-generated income, plus equipment and fund split, sales and merchandising.

- **Decision-making and authority** Details the various decisions that will need unanimous approval from all band members. Such issues should cover usage of band income and assignment of any rights. Can also detail how much goes in the kitty, what it's used for, who decides, who has access and where it's kept!

- **Membership changes** Explains the process of band changes, which will require reasonable notice and unanimous consent.

- **Use of band names** Should ideally state that the band name is vested in the band so any member leaving would not be entitled to take the name with them. This may not always be the case as a member may be precious about the name if they came up with it. It would be in the band's interest to convince them otherwise.

- **Rehearsals and performance** Should oblige each member to commit enough time for studio and live events. Any consistent breach could result in that member being asked to leave.

- **Side projects** Will allow members to work with other bands subject to defined rules, barriers and resolutions.

A simple agreement written between the group is fine, although the final copy should be drawn up or checked by a music lawyer. Add or exclude anything you like, cover as much as possible and make sure everyone agrees to stick to it.

Signing a formal agreement makes it harder for anyone to go against the group decision, and also helps to highlight potential problems and focus the goals and aims of the band.

Regardless of whether the band is run by one individual or by group decision, an agreement between all members prevents future misunderstandings and provides guidelines in the event of a dispute. Always get someone independent to witness your signatures when signing the agreement.

## Why have an agreement?

There are websites out there with loads and loads of how to information. Most of it is American and most of it from a legal perspective. And most of it is total bollocks. **The only thing that really kills bands is ego.** It's never a good thing when egos step into a band as that will spell the end of the dream. I don't think it's really necessary for a band to draw up an agreement stating who the leader is or who is in charge. If it's got to that point then you are already in trouble. But it is worth pointing out what the basics of band agreements should do.

Just be aware that you will go through a baptism of fire when your music takes off and all of a sudden everything becomes very real. Money is getting made, in some cases a lot of money, and attention is being paid to some members more than others. Whether you think you can stick it now doesn't matter. I'm telling you it's impossible to prepare for the kind of madness that a band will go though when that success button has been hit. This is when having a good team of people around you will matter more than anything you can buy. And having those band agreements sorted out and discussed, before the green-eyed monster enters carrying its horde of cash and other so-called delights that await some of you, is best done sooner than later. The days when it was really your band against the world will be over, your innocence lost and each member blooded in battle.

# Writing Good Songs

iii

Thou shall write thy songs and spread the word

Commandment Three

While you can study what makes a song good it's a whole different thing to write a good song. In their career most bands have a period where all their great hits happen and then it diminishes. That's the nature of the musical beast. And then there are some bands who never really hit their potential. The definition of a good song is: one that always

> **The definition of a good song is one that always takes you back to where you were when you first heard it...**

takes you back to where you were when you first heard it. It can bring back memories, smells, and feelings and that's what makes a song timeless. Perhaps there could be a magic formula to writing hit songs, but the surest way to writing a good song is to simply keep writing them.

## FINDING OUT WHAT MAKES A GOOD SONG

I think it's worth studying songs from as many genres as you can, from the early 1930s to present day. Listen to as many old radio style stations as you can and get away from what was the top 40. Make compilation CDs from many different acts and make sure you go outside of your own musical preferences. I get asked all the time what a record label is looking for and the only answer any A&R guy will give is songs. Listen to Elvis (though he never wrote any of his, but still a great example of songwriting), the Beatles, the Rolling Stones, Mammas and Pappas, Jimi Hendrix, Duran Duran along with other acts from the 80s up until Oasis, Radiohead and Coldplay. The point is to make as diverse a compilation as you can and study:

- song structure
- intros and outros
- melodies
- chord structure
- verse
- mid sections

and dissect everything about the song.

This is what you are up against and competing with. The more songs you listen to the more you will develop your song worldliness. And whilst some songs writers are born with a natural instinct, songwriting can be developed. There are numerous books and courses on songwriting which can be handy. But the most important thing that these courses cannot give is individuality. When you hear a song you can instantly place it with either the band or songwriter. Too much rule following may take that magic away. So, take what you need and let your talent do the rest.

## Collaborating

Of course, when it comes to bands, collaboration helps hugely in developing songwriting potential. If it was good enough for the Beatles, then who are you to argue. Radiohead are another example of collaboration and, whilst Noel Gallagher is one of the best songwriters of his generation, Oasis again exemplify how a band can redefine itself when other members are brought in to share the writing, as the band did on later albums.

## Creative songwriting

When it comes to songwriting many acts don't seem to really think too deeply about what they are doing. It's as if they take for granted that they are already great songwriters. If any of you are reading this wondering why you haven't been signed yet, it's because your songwriting talent has let you down. Whether it's the title of the song, the lyric or melody, many bands tend to think they have just written a definite hit. Which is really not the case. I often wonder when I hear new music from unsigned bands what has gone through their heads when writing the song. Most of the time it's just inexperience in songwriting that lets bands down, and if they are open to guidance some bands do improve. If you dissect what a song is it gives you a better understanding of how to write better songs in the future. Most of all, you need to have imagination. No imagination equals zero magic. And whilst I would not pretend to offer a course in songwriting there are some things you can take into consideration.

- Songs can be broken down into their structure.

- Songs are alive, they have a heartbeat all of their own. They reach out and demand to be heard.

- They have set patterns and elements that can be divided into different ingredients.

A formula for a song might be as follows.

# THE SONG

## The title

Eagerly reading the title of your favourite band's new album, along with the track listing in a magazine or website, is the first salvo that fires the imagination when it comes to songs. Song titles make statements. They sell the song and make you want to hear it. Song titles like Iron Maiden's *Hallowed be Thy Name* or Radiohead's *Paranoid Android* or Oasis's *Don't Look Back in Anger* are strong titles that fill you with expectancy. I'm not going to emphasise the boring aspect of a song title so let's say that out of 40 songs to listen to, the stronger song titles like *Sympathy for the Devil* or *Live and Let Die* would jump out to be heard first. Same with album titles, which one would you go for, *Definitely Maybe, Never Mind the Bollocks* or *Watching Paint Dry?* There are so many songs out in the world these days that the song title will be the first selling point. It will be the Zen of the song. So make it interesting.

## The lyric

Lyrics can be ambiguous or they can be definitive. It's a relative thing to the individual to discern what a song means. Some Oasis tracks, by Noel Gallagher's own admission, could have been better written, but they don't suffer because the lyrics fit perfectly with the music and vocal line and so the message of the song comes across. Some songs are really just dumb rock and roll. But you are still left satisfied. And that is part of the Oasis charm. As a band they tapped into the heartbeat of their generation better than any band really since the Rolling Stones. The danger and excitement they caused as a band, as songwriters, despite the seemingly relative simplicity of their songs, typify what good songs are all about. Don't for one second think Oasis songs are easy to write. Try writing six hit albums and numerous hit b-sides and let me know how you get on. And in this day and age that is quite a feat.

Lyrics should have meaning. They should say something. They should be a mini soap opera of the emotional kind. Lyrics can be simplistic or you can weave a poetic tapestry. Do your lyrics flow? Can the listener follow the words line by line? Do the lyrics have a developing theme and interesting resolution leading to a satisfying artistic statement that connects to the heart? Does each verse build towards a momentum?

Think about the songs you love and why you love them. The main reason anyone likes a song is because it catches on to something inside you. They come to mean something to you. Remember the sound track to your life? Most songs are based on love for a reason. Everyone falls in and out of love all the time. And they will till our governments blow us all to hell. Any time you get dumped by your lover there is always a song that comes along to kick you some more in the teeth. There is always a song somewhere that echoes exactly how you are feeling. Because songwriters have gone through the emotions you are going through, but have made an artistic statement of what they are feeling and somewhere on Earth someone is feeling the same way. Songs are anthems, they are love songs, they are protest songs, they are songs of hope and most of all they are songs of love. The song has to reach out and make you go 'oh my God!'. Next time you get ready for a Friday night out and you blast The Cult's *Fire Woman* on your stereo, it's because it's filling you with a surge of adrenalin that is better than any drug known to any living soul. That is where songs touch us as people. In our souls.

## The melody

Great melodies stick in your mind. The tune of a song releases endorphins that resonate throughout your entire being. The concept of a good melody is simplistic but to define it is truly complex. Sitting down to write a simple song is hugely difficult. They either flow or they take weeks to write. The main staple of a melody is the energy of the music. Does the energy flow? Does it fuel the song? Are there bits in the song that dip? Is a time change needed? Does the time change affect the energy of the song in a negative way? The melody of the song is the engine. If you write a melody that someone hums back to you a day or a week later then you have a hit on your hands. Listening to stacks of music in A&R meetings it's the melodies that come back to me a week later from the bands that I know who have what it takes.

It's not always that you get a song straightaway, some songs take a while to grow. And then sometimes there are songs that don't follow the normal rules. Typically bands have verse, chorus, verse, chorus, midsection, etc. This is monotonous when it comes to hearing so much music. The bands that break those rules and become a little more inventive in their approach are the ones that stand out.

## THE KEY TO SONGWRITING

These are just basic principles. The key to songwriting doesn't really lie in formulas or rules, otherwise you would end up sounding just like every other artist out there. But basic principles are worth considering when it comes to analysing songs. During my time in A&R most bands I got through followed the verse, chorus, verse chorus, midsection, verse, chorus routine. It doesn't make it very interesting when you are looking at what is supposed to be the best of the unsigned music scene. If you sound like everyone else then you will not set the imagination on fire and then it's back to the drawing board.

When you are thinking about writing songs it's worth trusting what your instinct is saying. You can read all the books in the world and be taught by the best songwriters but this will never guarantee you will follow in their footsteps. Get out your guitar and play. Write every day and set your standards high. You are up against the best in the world and your biggest judges will not be the record labels, it will be the public. I researched a few articles over the internet that went into the science of songwriting but it all sounded very American. I really believe most musicians can write good songs and even one or two great ones. But the art of songwriting in itself comes from within. It's one of those X-factor things, you either have it or you don't.

# The Importance of Rehearsals

iv

Thou shall rehearse like Demons

Commandment Four

Rehearsals are more important than some bands and artists think. They are the first real step to the live performance and it's where you smooth the edges out when it comes to performing the songs in the live arena. I've gone to see bands in rehearsals sitting around smoking weed and drinking like it's party time. Whilst there is a time and place for it, rehearsals isn't it. This automatically created a bad impression along with it being naive on many levels. Getting high does not give you the best results when it comes to either playing or rehearsing. It affects your hearing and makes you sloppy. Subsequently when it comes to the live performance these bands don't cut it. So, leave party time to party time and be professional always. The life of any band is vastly reduced when drink and drugs enter their lives.

## THE INS AND OUTS OF REHEARSING

Every town in the UK will have a rehearsal studio and whilst rates vary the money you have just saved by not getting high will pay for your rehearsal time. Most bands or artists just starting out should aim to rehearse three to five times per week. You should compare yourself to an Olympic athlete when it comes to rehearsing. The live performance is the single biggest aspect a band has. If you don't deliver when it comes to a show then the band in rehearsal studio number two who spend all their time practising are the ones who get the success.

Rehearsals should be approached like you are doing the show, only without an audience watching. This gets you into a mindset where every time you play, you are doing so to deliver the performance of your life. That way, when it comes to a gig you don't need to switch into a mindset that isn't natural. **A performance is always a performance, whether two people or 200 are watching you.**

## Using rehearsal studies

Most rehearsal studios these days are professional and will have a room where you can record your performance. This is worth doing and playing back to see where any weak areas crop up. Rehearse the entire set and just let the recorder run. A video camera is handy to record rehearsals to see how you all look. Is there any shoe-gazing going on? Do you all look bored? Or is there a fire, a passion that runs through the band when playing? These are tools to help you maximise your performance and deliver the best possible gig live. It's also a must to incorporate a click track into your rehearsals. Playing to a click track will completely hone your performance and tighten the band's sound to a very professional level. You will be surprised how sloppy you may sound compared to when you have practised to a click track. Any band I've ever come across that sounds amazingly tight cut it because they have the discipline to incorporate every tool into their armoury. You all must have seen bands play that sound all over the place. No click track equals a sloppy and undisciplined band.

## A&R AND REHEARSALS

An A&R guy may request to come to a rehearsal. Some managers aren't keen on this as it becomes a showcase for the record company. But I think it's worthwhile. Bands should not be precious as things can go wrong at gigs and you can control a rehearsal environment. At gigs chaos can reign and you have to prepare for the unexpected. I saw a band once at the Water Rats venue in Kings Cross in London. The particular manager was a tad precious about the band she was managing and everything had to be perfect. The problem with that is this is rock and roll and the Gods of Chaos decided to pay a visit. There were a lot of industry present that night, but no one would go near the stage. And then an old granny walked in after having a few too many hot cocoas laced with brandy. The band were in the middle of rocking out when this dear sweet old lady went to the front of the stage and proceeded to produce her gravity-affected breasts to the disbelief of everyone present. The sight was so surreal nobody could take the band seriously at that point and the gig was over.

If A&R do want to pop along to see you rehearse take the opportunity and make sure you are well rehearsed and ready. If they like you they will come to a gig and already you are developing a rapport. I've seen bands in rehearsals and it's a good chance to sit with the band and listen to the songs before moving on to the next level. You can expect a lot of A&R activity at rehearsals when it comes to record company interest. You will be doing a lot of showcase events for the interested label and it's a good way to get used to what can be a very dry environment.

## SCALING DOWN

To finalise on this subject, bands and artists should start to scale down rehearsal time after four to six months of hard slog. There is such a thing as being to slick and too polished. You do need too keep an edge so keep the practice to no fewer than one to two per week. Obviously when it comes a tour you ramp up the rehearsal time again until you have ironed out any weakness before going on to play those first notes in anger.

# Going on Tour

Commandment Five

The basis of any band's life is gigging. If you gig once in a blue moon you may as well quit. No excuses can be accepted at all if you do not take this as the holy grail of a band's existence. You live to play. Jobs, family, relationships or lack of money should never be used to justify why you are not playing every month. Or to be more realistic, to average it out over a year you should aim to play a minimum of 30 gigs a year. Playing live is the cornerstone of building a fan-base and your profile. Being stuck in a rehearsal room will only make you jaded. So, you either get onto booking a round of gigs every two months, or go full flight and get yourself onto a tour.

## CREATING A TOUR

There are so many bands now you can buddy up with other bands and create tours around the UK. For example, if you are already headlining your own home town and doing good elsewhere then book a tour using local support acts to bring in the audience. And then, repay the favour. This would help out so many bands across the UK to build a good audience and help out the music scene in every town. It's really a no-brainer, but many bands don't understand this. Even if it's just weekends, you still have Fri, Sat and Sun to make a noise. Venues exist to have bands play and get people in through the doors. They want you to succeed, because if you don't neither do they.

A few years ago when tribute bands were all the rage it was hard for a regular, original band to get a gig on the weekends as this was when the venue had a chance to make the money needed to keep them afloat. And whilst this still holds true it seems the tribute scene isn't quite so dominant as it once was. Still, playing with a tribute act linked to your style of music is a great way to expose yourselves to a new audience. Otherwise it's a case of getting on to bands in every town in the UK and saying hello.

## The buddy system

The band buddy buddy system is the way forward. Everyone wins. And whilst there will always be egos involved, with bands wanting to blow each other off the stage, having this mentality will only serve to harm you. Leave the ego stuff where it belongs and get together to put on shows. As far as the industry is concerned, you don't count. As far as the audience is concerned, they just want to hear the music. As far as the venue is concerned, they just want people in through the doors. So, as far your egos are concerned, leave that to when you have a private jet. I've seen management meetings turn to farce due to egos being present and all it accomplished was disagreements and bad blood. It contributed nothing to the tour or all-round good feeling and I think in the end it just diminishes what could be a very cool time on the road.

## Promoting a tour

To a point promoters will do what they can to help bands out. It's always in their interests. A tour can be anything from a week to months out on the road playing your heart out, eating pot noodles and living like gypsies. If you tour in support of a new release then you will need someone who is organised to do all the arranging. There really is no point in booking a gig in Inverness for one night and then somewhere in Cornwall the next. And yet I have seen some bands do this!

## BOOKING A TOUR

I would recommend you start off slowly. Book a series of gigs around your regional area and start to widen the net. Promoters book months in advance now, so I would confirm the towns you want to play first. Give yourself enough time to arrange those gigs close to each other when you speak to the venue and then enquire to see which dates are available. Thinking ahead four months will save you a lot of headaches and organising when it comes to sorting the tour out. Bands have complained that it's really hard to get a gig in London, for instance, due to the need to get people in through the door. Well, here's a secret, it's the same in every town. This problem isn't limited to good old Londinium, it's a problem most venues face and of course what most bands are left dealing with. That's where the buddy buddy system comes into place.

## How to arrange a tour

Pick ten towns. Then hit the venues in those towns to check availability.

Make sure you have your website sorted out with all the info anyone needs to know who you are. Have tracks available to listen to and an email for contact. When you speak to a promoter they will either want to hear the stuff on the website or get you to send a CD.

If you have the option in a new town always go for a first or second slot. The local town band will bring the crowd and you don't want to play after them as everyone will amble off home.

As an alternative you can access the local music website and place an ad requesting to support one of the more popular bands in return for them supporting you. I would make a list of the ten coolest bands in each town you want to play and then get in contact. If you make friends this way it will make life easier to book a tour. In the directory there will be a list of each town's local music portal.

Set up a page on your website asking bands who want to play where you are to organise a gig where they are and vice versa. Then you place your advert on the websites and await the response. This all sounds rather simple, but I've seen it in action and it works rather well. In the absence of a music agent this will be a lot of work but it's worth the payoff.

The more organised and professional you are the better chance you have of getting that mini-tour booked.

To summarise:

1) Choose ten towns.

2) Contact the ten coolest bands from those towns.

3) Contact them and organise gig swaps.

4) They book gigs and get you to support, then you book gigs and get them to support.

5) Let the promoter know this is what you are doing, they will see the sense in it.

6) Once the gigs are confirmed, email your mailing list and organise press activity.

7) Contact the university press and media.

8) Contact the local paper news column.

9) Place music from all the bands on your website and advertise the tour.

10) Once you have done all this, go back and do it again.

## PRESS AND PROMOTION

Going out on the road can be an expensive business. So start slow and then build. There is no point in doing any of this if you don't do the work behind it. That means press and promotion. Always make sure you have songs available for kids to hear. Promoters are now including web addresses in their mailouts for people to check out the bands. This is the only way to do it. It lets people have the chance to hear the music before heading out to a gig. And if there are four bands playing there's a good chance they will like one out of four. When they attend the gig they will mostly stay the entire night and who knows, you may well win a fan or two.

## UKBANDS.NET

One company taking the touring issue that huge step forward is **www.ukbands.net** who have launched a touring service that takes the heartache out of touring and will give you that bit more of a professional edge. Cost is the single biggest factor, whether you play one gig or 20, and it is often that which decides how often a band can play and indeed where. But the rock and roll life of a band is not for the fainthearted, and if all you do is moan and groan about how hard and expensive it all is, then it's time to jack it in and get a real job.

But what if you had an opportunity for a company that could organise all of this for you? Someone who could professionally take care of all the business side and leave you to just rehearse and prepare for the live shows, would you do it?

## What's the benefit?

www.ukbands.net have come up with one of the best services I never thought would happen on this level. UKB live concerts have a touring package that blew my mind when I first heard about it. I think what has impressed me is that we now have a company that is really taking things to the next level. It's almost saying to the bands, 'OK, if you want to do this then let's do it properly.' It's almost a challenge to bands to put their money where their mouth is. And I know already there are many bands who spend all day hitting websites and moaning about how much they hate the music industry. Well, here in this book the onus is all on you to make that music career work, without the industry you hate so much affecting you directly.

You will always need professional services and that's why it's going to be very interesting to see how this touring service develops. I will add that bands only moan because nobody really pays them any attention, and like a little doggy they do nothing but bark and cry in the night until someone tells them to shut up. Well my friends, here we are, here is a service that's open to you and I'm going to challenge you all to get on the road and see how good you really are.

## The deal

The full cost and benefits of the UKB Touring Agency is as follows.

- UKbands touring package: cost £329 per person. This may sound like a lot of money up front but when you consider the benefits on offer I think it is good value. This is what you get:

- The five-day tour schedule:

    - double decker tour coach and backline trailer for five days

    - five premier UK shows in five premier locations

    - four elite after-show parties and guests

    - one professional tour manager.

- Professional backline techs.

- National media advertisements.

- Regional press coverage as well as press interviews with the artists.

- All graphics for tour including high quality press releases, web adverts, MySpace and UKB profile graphics.

- Constant UKB advertisements on the mailouts for over 200,000 recipients.

- Live photo shoot and backstage promo shots.

- DVD shoot.

- Full tour production including all access laminate passes, tour itinerary booklets and full UKB branding at the events with tour backdrops and band info flyers.

You are paying for a service that includes full press and publicity, organisation and you even get a DVD made from the tour, which you can sell on your website. This is a total professional service that you would expect if you were already a signed band doing the business with a record deal. And don't forget that a lot of these initial costs are tax deductible.

The beauty of this approach is that you are paying someone else to organise and execute a tour for you. If I was in a band, I'd sign up right away. The fact that you can also get a DVD shot from the time you are on the road is a valuable income stream. So, whilst for some bands the initial outlay of £329 each may seem steep, when in fact it isn't, the money you could potentially recoup far outweighs any expense. I'm giving this the full Rock and Roll Times seal of approval.

# Creating and Using a Website

Everyone knows how important websites are to bands. It has to be in the top three of getting things done before you enter the public arena. MySpace has become the phenomenon of the digital age showing how good and how bad bands, as well as regular people, can be. I've noticed a lot of bands focus more on their MySpace accounts than their website and I think this has been to the detriment of the band's progress, or at least to its organisation. MySpace is a great platform for telling people who you are and what you are up to. But that's where it ends. Your purpose is to interact with your fans. And I think MySpace fails in that regard. People are so busy trying to look cool, adding countless numbers of friends to their accounts, that they fail to see it does not translate into any positive action. How boring is it really to read 'thanks for adding us'? Bands sometimes spend two or three hours a day looking to be added or adding people to their MySpace site and leaving their poor old band website to turn into a ghost town. This has got to stop.

## MYSPACE VERSUS A WEBSITE

Anyone can add a truckload of names to a website, so what! And if you really believe having thousands of friends on your MySpace account matters, then you are sadly deluded. How many of those friends have attended one of your gigs, bought your CD or a T-shirt? Yeah, maybe one or two, but you have thousands of friends, right? Do you still have to get up in the morning to get to a job you hate? Oh you do, so why haven't all those friends supported you then? Why haven't they bought the CD, gone to a gig or bought your T-shirt? It's because the whole thing is a total fallacy.

What you want are fans, not friends. Whilst friends may tell you how great you are, which is only good for your ego, fans buy CDs. Fans buy T-shirts and fans come to your gigs. This translates into you having money and a sustainable career where you finally give up that much hated job and have become self-sufficient through playing music. That's what you are doing this for, right? And any A&R guy that puts emphasis on your MySpace friends list is playing a very dangerous game indeed, because it is no safety net. They will expect to see you play with all these great friends you have and when no one turns up at your gig, and if it's not about the music, it will only serve to harm the band. I've heard A&R guys spout on about how the band must be great if they have loads of friends. This is really scary. Once you hear the music from these bands there is no way in hell they have that many mates.

## Beware of 'friends'

This leads to a conclusion that the band in question must have generated a lot of friends to make them look good. If that's the case it only proves that any band can then do that with the know-how, making the whole exercise redundant. I know one band in particular who have so much money they can pay people to go round getting added. I would love to tell you who it is, but that would only serve their egotistical purpose. So let's put it this way, if you have to buy everything to make you look good, and that includes getting onto tours, getting your video played, into magazines, into people's lives, then you are very sad. Music will change people's lives and if your music is good enough, people will pay you to play it.

MySpace is easy to set up, it's all done for you. It takes no creativity, and you look and sound like every other band out there. You have essentially become part of a corporate conveyor belt with no imagination. But hey, you have thousands of friends, right? I've said enough about that particular site. Let's focus on what you really should be doing.

## YOUR WEBSITE

A website doesn't have to be the flashiest or coolest thing out there. It just needs to be functional. The basic requirement for a website is to interact with your fan base. And all you need for that is as follows.

### Who you are

A bio section containing the history of the band along with individual sections on each member.

### Pictures

Pictures from either live shows or staged. People want to know what bands look like and all you need are a few shots. You can even take them with your mobile phone.

### Media

I would place four of your best songs here. Three songs for streaming and one for download. If you have an album it is worth streaming bits from each song as an enticer for sale. If you have a video available then this is the section to place it in.

### News

Keep this section as current as you can. Not even the big boys can keep this bit running 24/7, but when you are playing live or there is plenty of activity then this is your portal to the world.

### Gigs

Always make sure you give the correct information. Place the name, address, website and phone number of the venue you are playing. Almost every band will have fans under the age of 18 and it's worth mentioning if any venues you are playing run an over-18 policy only.

## Forum

I think forums are a good idea. It gets the fans interacting with each other, gets your band talked about and in some sections you can arrange transportation to gigs for the kids. This is where the community really works.

## Email lists

Collecting emails is a must. You need to have on your site an email section where fans can enter their details, along with collecting them at gigs. It's worth having the admin details of which town your fans are from. That way when you play a gig in that town, you have a captured audience. Make sure you only send out email news when it's relevant. Otherwise you end up sending news out that no one really wants to hear. When you send out news to your mailing list limit the user groups to no more than 20-30 recipients, otherwise your ISP may think you are spamming and close you down. News to be included should be upcoming gigs, releases, and any mention of press activity.

## Merchandise

You will need a section to sell T-shirts and CDs. Paypal is a good way to administer the financial aspects and keep everything nice and safe. UKbands (**www.ukbands.net**) have launched a site where you can have a band webpage to take care of this for you. You can place a link to their site which takes care of the business elements. On the band webpage you will have a section regarding who the band is, with your merch and CD for sale. Some bands do find it a hassle to organise a section that takes care of selling their wares and if you can get someone else to do this for you it is worth considering. UKbands have a subscription rate that runs into the hundreds of thousands so can deal with the bandwidth.

That's really all you need to do to make your website effective. If money starts to flow in, or you have someone who is a web genius, then you can make the site as creative as you like.

# Merch Hell

Merchandise is a very important income stream for a band. The way things are shaping with record deals and recoupment it seems that most bands will make more money from T-shirt sales and touring than selling CDs. And that can be the same whether you are signed or not. People love clothes and if you are a fan of a band then you will be buying merch. So, this has to be part of your battle plan. Looking at various merchandise companies it seems that they will do deals and match prices or undercut competitors which means a great deal for the band. In fact it seems all a bit too cut throat for me. However, what you want is to make friends with a company who do not do minimum orders. Most merch companies will out-do and out-bid everyone else so there is no real excuse for not getting the best deal you can.

## BEYOND THE T-SHIRT

I think bands need to start getting away from the regular standardised T-shirt and start thinking a lot more creatively. Obviously it does go without saying that the T-shirt sales will be your bread and butter when it comes to merchandise, but with a little thought bands could create a clothing line that differentiates them from the competition. It took a while for the merchandise industry to realise that fans will buy anything with their favourite band's name on it. Some of those things are good and some bad, with some big name bands selling anything they can think of. It reminds me of an episode of *The Simpsons* where Krusty the Clown wholeheartedly endorsed any product with his name on it.

Some big American bands have gone down that road, to the point where they even charge their fans a truckload of money to spend five minutes with them (along with condoms, coffins and coffee!), when they should really be releasing a new album. The name of that band begins with K and ends with iss. This is taking it too far and really is a classless act. This is just an example of a band turning into a corporation and making money for the sake of it. You, however, are going to be creating something that hopefully will be looked at as something very cool and special.

## Market your image

Remember what I said about bands being a gang? If you are the type of band with an image, then market that image. Capitalise on what it is that makes you special. If you have seen the film *The Warriors* then you will know what it's all about. I'm not glorifying the violence but the look of the film is what I'm saying. Fashion, whether you like it or not, is part of a band. Not having an image is still an image. You are still making a statement. And if you have an artistic member of the band who creates art then let them loose on designing the band's style. If you don't have an artistic member then find someone and rope them in. If you are at college or university you will know someone doing an art class. Utilise your surroundings. If you can't pay anyone then offer free entry to gigs, CDs or cut a deal. The reality is that most people offered a chance to highlight their talents will do so.

The point is to have something unique to your band that differs from everyone else. Take a look at any local music scene website and you get the same bands with the same looks and the same-sounding, tired songs. Bands need to create a sound and look that jumps out and demands to be heard and seen. Otherwise you really are just another group coming off the conveyer belt.

## TYPES OF MERCHANDISE

As you start out of course the main items will be T-shirts. But have a think about designing them so they are more than average. It's up to you to be creative in this. Swear words, etc have already been done and I think people have become a little bit more sophisticated than to be shocked by it anymore. If the cover design for your CD looks special then that's the first thing to go for. Tour dates on the back of the T-shirt are old hat so maybe something else is cooler. Your website address for instance contains more info than past gig dates.

Caps, hats, wristbands and hoodies are the mainstay for bands starting out in merchandise. I would stay away from stickers, etc as this always smacks of desperation when bands' sticker everywhere. They get old fast and bring nothing back to the band. So don't go wasting money thinking placing a sticker on a wall somewhere will do you any good. I have yet to see any evidence this works so invest your money in the things that work. Saying that, if the band has a very cool logo it's worth getting a template knocked up to sell to the fans. It would be far cooler for a new fan to be able to spray your band logo on their guitar case, bedroom wall, car or budgie.

## Generating income

Once you have decided on the types and styles of merch you then have a potential source of income to sell over the internet and at gigs. If you win new fans playing live then you will sell T-shirts, hats, posters, bags and even your granny. People will always buy clothes and fans will always buy merchandise from their favourite artists. It's down to you to make it as cool as you like. It's also up to you to define your own definition of cool.

There are many things a band can do when it comes to selling something new. You don't tend to see any kind of tour diaries out there. I'd be interested to read a band's tour diary, where they played, to how many people, what the gig was like, how long the tour was, what kind of press and promo activities the band had to go through, how bad the hotel/bus/tent was, etc. You could add all kinds of pictures from the tour. And it would be another way of connecting with the fans. It would just be a cool and interesting insight to life on the road. Merchandise can bring in a lot of money. Just ask George Lucas!

# Enter the Studio

Commandment Six

Seven years ago I was still getting demos sent into the office on cassette tapes. Around about the year 2001 bands started submitting music on CD and the cassette was dead. And with it low quality recordings. The ante was upped inside a year and everything changed. Most bands can now record music that is commercially ready for sale. And once again it's about being up against other artists, so submitting any CD with badly recorded music will automatically kill your chances of an A&R guy taking it any further.

## RECORDING YOURSELF

There has been no better time for bands. The end result for any band wanting a career is to record albums. The digital age has given bands the freedom to record top quality music for relatively little finance. Computer recorded music has enabled any musician wanting a career to build mini recording studios using computers in their bedrooms. Digital recording programs like Pro Tools, Sonar, Cubase and Reason have freed musicians from a bondage that even five years ago seemed out of reach. The financial cost of PCs has come within the reach of everyone and an investment of £1,000 would give you a top quality computer with a digital music software program. So there is no excuse for bands to not get recordings done.

However, like anything, the expertise in getting those music programs to do the job they were designed to do takes practice. Having a laptop loaded up with Pro Tools or any preferred music software program should be the first tool a band invests in when getting started. Taking the laptop to rehearsals and gigs to record performances is the first step in pre-production. **If you are serious about what you do then the laptop should be attached to the band's hip at all times.**

## USING RECORDING STUDIOS

Recording studios are still expensive, but as they are facing a hard time adapting to current trends deals can be made. It's worth calling a studio up for a chat to see what kind of deal you can get.

Most studios will have down time where you may get a chance to record for a reduction in fees. This tends to be late at night, very early in the morning or early in the week. Weekends will be booked up as this will be when most bands are free. All studios will have show reels of bands they have recorded and this is the first step to take to check out the quality of the studio. The studio engineer should have no problems with providing you with a copy of the bands they have worked on.

Take the CDs home and have a listen. If the recordings sound good at home then you have a good chance at getting a good CD recorded for your band. The days of bands recording demos are over. Since digital technology took over I haven't really had a demo in the office. I have had low quality recordings, but this is more down to the studio and its facilities than anything else. Like I mentioned, most bands can release their CDs commercially and this is the mindset you need to have before you enter the studio. Your aim is to capture the music for sale at gigs and over the internet. Do not accept anything less. And before you ask how much money this will take I have heard CDs that cost £500 pounds to record that I would happily buy as a quality end product.

## Looking for a studio

When you go to scout a studio the basic requirements should be:

- the recording facilities
- effects
- what the recording engineer is like
- whether the studio has a separate drum and vocal booth
- all-round ambience.

The vibe of a studio has to work for you to capture the magic of the songs. If the studio is a dump then look elsewhere. A good sound engineer will sit down and explain the process and ask what experience you have had. Be honest and tell them if you haven't had any. This will save a lot of time messing around, which costs you money.

When it comes to recording the songs there are a few basic ways of doing so. And this really boils down to the type of band you are and style of music. You will find what works for you and what makes you comfortable. It should go without saying that you do not enter a studio until you have the songs rehearsed and you know them backwards. Recording songs that have not been fully thought through and rehearsed to a professional standard will expose weakness and cause delays that will eat into the expensive studio time you have paid for. This can ruin a potentially good recording session and is a lesson that does not need to be learned the hard way.

## LIVE RECORDING

Recording your songs 'live' – as if you were performing at a gig – allows you to retain the energy of performance and is the quickest way if you are an experienced band or singer. However, this is more suited to bluesy type bands and doesn't really give you any options to experiment with the songs or make them dynamic. Also, it doesn't really capture the essence of what recording a song is all about. You could stick a mini disc onto the sound desk at a gig and get the same result. It's ok if you want to release a live album, but then if you release a live album, you may as well turn it into live performance DVD. Live albums are a very boring concept from the 70s, before technology gave us all the chance to record a killer live concert on film. Stay away from releasing live performance CDs. What's the point, DVD all the way.

## LAYERED RECORDING

Each instrument is recorded separately, often to a click track or guide vocal – much slower but produces more professional results, better for newcomers but far more expensive due to the extra time taken. However, this gives you the option to explore what a song is capable of, such as adding extra dimensions to a track or filling the sound out with extra guitar parts and vocal harmonies. Digital technology adds spice by having access to thousands of effects.

However, as this is a creative process, unless you know what you are doing it is best to trust an experienced producer or sound engineer. It can be easy to get carried away and add all sorts of effects to a song. Keep it simple and as you progress you will learn how effective studio production can be. The song always comes first but studio production can add dynamics; like a great artist painting a picture it's knowing when to stop.

## Your budget

Costs range from an hourly rate to £100+ per day and you will have to include the mix-down time into your budget (anything from one hour to seven days depending on amount of tracks recorded and instruments used). As most studios have transferred over to digital technology you must make sure you get the digital source files or hard disk for future use. The amount of songs you can record will be determined by the budget you have to spend. It is worth saving as much as you can and if that means waiting an extra month to do the best job you can, you should. You can press an album for sale at gigs, which should be considered for the next recording.

Before you get into the next stage of recording, which is mastering the tracks, you need to get the songs mixed.

## MIXING

Top bands can take up to two weeks to mix down a track. It's a subject that can take an entire book in itself to explain, with many audio courses that teach you the complete science of how to mix music. But the point is with the software available to bands it can be done at home. There is never a substitute for a top-class producer/mixer when it comes to getting the job done properly, but that doesn't mean to say you cannot do a good job yourself when it comes to recording your own material. It's still a huge learning process but one worth learning as you will only gain experience from actually doing it. And with top studios going out of business there's a lot less chance for young kids to learn their craft with professionals.

So don't be afraid of getting stuck in and learning what it takes. The recording studio software will have all the necessary magic for you to mix good tracks. Don't get caught up in the alchemy of mixing either. If you can read, have an open mind, follow instructions and have passion, you will be able to sit down and learn how to mix.

## What is mixing?

Mixing is the process by which you place each recorded part of the song together to form the song itself. When you mix a track you are adjusting the volumes, pan positions and frequency of all the recorded tracks. You are essentially blending all the tracks together to complete the final song. The basic overview for this is to start with the drums and then build, adding the guitars, bass and then vocals. You can then add all sorts of extra parts that will bring magic to a song. Mixing is balancing the song together so the parts fit. This is where you can add a multitude of effects. Bands should ensure that they capture the essence of the song from the start. It can be easy to think any weakness can be fixed when it comes to mixing and, whilst you can add magic to a song in the mix down, and let's face it most bands do this, it can take away from the song at the same time. Just make sure you are totally rehearsed beforehand and get the best performance you can from the beginning. You can then add all sorts of extras and effects once the ground work has been complete.

Mixing has become a fashionable buzz word, with mixing engineers commanding huge sums for remixing tracks. But ultimately a good mix is a perfect balance of instrument levels, creating a sonic rollercoaster ride with each instrument blended to perfection, giving the listener a satisfying experience.

## APPROACHING THE RECORDING SESSION

With the production process in mind I asked music producer Richard Robson some questions regarding how bands should approach the recording sessions. Richard started out at

Metropolis Studios in London before branching out into free-lance production. As a writer, programmer and producer Richard has worked with the Rolling Stones, Richard Ashcroft, Dido, Jeff Beck and The Longcut amongst others.

### What is the music producer's role within the band?

The producer usually ends up being a little bit of everything required to get the production completed. This can include creative and musical ideas and direction, accounting and time management skills, engineer, musician, after dinner speaker, making the tea, cleaner, cab driver, and providing emotional support and marriage/relationship counselling. I'm sure there are some more that I've missed...

### What should bands understand about the production process?

This really depends on the level of involvement that the band wants to have. As long as the band are happy with the results of the production process it's not crucial for them to understand what is happening 'behind the scenes'. The focus of the process should be to produce the best possible results from the material the band are creating, and to help them realise their artistic goals. Faith in the producer's abilities is a crucial, but the band has to pick the right producer at the outset.

### Do music producers mix the tracks too?

Each producer will have their own unique system for completing the mixes. Often producers will mix the tracks, although many producers have no real hands-on mixing skills and will use an engineer to help them achieve the mix they are looking for. This can be the most pressured part of the production process as it's the last point at which ideas can be formed and changed, with deadlines to stick to and the recording budget reaching its end.

### Is the producer an added member of the band?

Sometimes the producer has a close relationship with the band, particularly if they are also playing within the band, although a more common role is as an external voice that helps the band understand how the music sounds to the listener, and how to cultivate that sound.

### How should bands approach a producer?

Bands shouldn't be afraid to go direct to the producer's management or representatives with a CD. MySpace is also a good way to make contact with a producer and allows you to hear some material and start to build a relationship with the band outside of the studio. Inviting a prospective producer to a show is also a good way to get to know the band, and can be the key to understanding how the sound of the band should be developed.

### Can a good producer make all the difference to a band?

The right producer can help a band develop and focus their sound, as well as helping the band in picking the right songs and arrangements to create the best tracks they can. Conversely the wrong producer can mask the qualities of the music and performances to make a potentially great track become very average. The producer's understanding and vision of the band's music is very important in turning what is a potentially great record into a great record.

### What does a producer look for in a band?

Charisma and great songs/lyrics as well as unique sounds and arrangements. Anything that sounds fresh and unusual will spark some interest. Other factors can usually be accommodated, but the core sound and a perceivable strength of commitment to the music are key.

### How should a band prepare before heading into the studio?

This is different from band to band. It usually helps if the band are sure of the material they're going to be recording and well rehearsed. It is often good to have a production meeting in advance so the band know what is going to be happening day-to-day in advance. Bring a spare of everything you can, and a huge bag of patience. Favourite personal distractions such as books, movies, iPods and video games, etc can help to eat up the time as the studio can involve a lot of waiting around.

For further info on Richard check out **www.record-producers.com/roster/richard-robson** and **www.myspace.com/freakmusicproductions**

## MASTERING

Mastering is the final stage in recording. This is the stage where the final mixes are presented and arranged in order for the album. The final mixes are polished to make ready for the master CD before it gets shipped to a pressing plant. The songs are treated with compression, adding dynamics and equalisation. The songs are brought together to make it sound like they belong on the same album. The sound levels are adjusted so you get consistency with frequency levels in each song balanced in comparison with the rest of the album. This will make the final mixes sound much more professional and louder without sacrificing any dynamics of the songs. Mastering will give your songs depth, punch and clarity and bring them to life. In every mastering session you can be sure a certain amount of actions will be performed:

- Songs will be optimised for average and peak volume levels.

- Signal processing with compression and EQ.

- Track listing and order with the timing between each song decided.

- Removal of any ghost sounds like hum, clicks, pops or hiss.

The process for an entire album can take between eight to 12 hours or around a ball park figure of an hour per song if the mixes are well recorded and no extra touches are needed.

## Online mastering

There are now online mastering services for bands to upload their mixes for mastering. The process is relatively quick, but each studio will work differently, and costs may vary slightly too. One studio is **www.masteringworld.com** who specialise in online mastering. Online mastering is a simple process of hitting the website and following the instructions. You will have a choice of engineer or studio depending on your requirements. You then pick what you need, pay the fees, upload your music according to what format the studio needs and off you go.

## A mastering engineer explains

I spoke to Donal Whelan from Masteringworld who explains what a mastering engineer does and what the process is perfectly. The two articles that follow really go in-depth about what you can expect from mastering. The first article guides you through the mastering process, leaving the second article to deal with the more technical aspects. Hope you enjoy, people!

This article first appeared on **www.soundnation.com** and is reproduced courtesy of **www.welshmusicfoundation.com**

Mastering is the final creative stage in the music production process. It's the process where your final mixes are compiled, polished and prepared ready for duplicating. There are a range of approaches to mastering, from compiling the album yourself with the aid of a few plug-ins, to going to London or New York and spending thousands of pounds in one of the legendary mastering facilities. In this article we'll explore some of the options, explode some of the myths, and help you coax the best out of your recordings before they go off to the factory.

### What does mastering do?

All commercial releases and most songs that you hear on the radio or clubs will have been mastered professionally. If your music is mastered well, it will stand side by side with other released CDs; if it is mastered badly or not mastered at all, it will sound out of place, or unfinished, or simply too quiet. Naturally, you will hear the difference mastering will make to your own music because you know it intimately, but other people, paradoxically, may not notice at all because it simply sounds right. With the massive technological advances that are happening every year, recording has become much more accessible to people outside the professional industry, to the point where it's now possible for a musician or an artist to record a whole album to a high quality in their bedroom or attic. It is arguably even more important therefore to put those projects through at least one professional stage before they are released to make sure that the final product sounds right, that there aren't any glaring errors that may have been overlooked on a smaller sound system, and that it will sound good on a variety of different sound systems.

### Should you master a demo?

Yes, if you want it to have impact when it's played by people in the industry, be they a booking agent or a manager or a record company employee. It's all a matter of degrees, but the better a product sounds and looks, the more likely it is to get noticed.

### Can your recording engineer master it for you?

Yes he can, and he probably has equipment that he can use to do it. However, he is intimately familiar with the music and he will probably master in the same room as he mixed your project, so you will be missing out on two important aspects of mastering

– a different (and often better) listening environment, and a fresh pair of ears with an impartial opinion. Most professional recording and mixing engineers prefer to pass on their work to an experienced mastering engineer for the final stage.

## PROFESSIONAL MASTERING

Professional mastering brings three important tools to bear on your music – the mastering studio, the mastering engineer, and the mastering gear. Mastering studios have carefully designed acoustics and excellent speakers. The mastering engineer needs these to make judgements on how a mix sounds, what needs to be done to the mix to make it sound right, and how it will translate to a variety of different systems when it has been released (for example a domestic hi-fi, a car stereo, the radio or a nightclub). It is more important to have a good and accurate listening environment in a mastering studio than it is in a recording studio. Recording engineers or mixing engineers need monitoring that they are comfortable with, that they can listen to for hours on end without getting fatigued, and that they know well enough to get a good mix on. Mastering engineers need flat, balanced monitoring so that they know that what they hear is true, and so that they can hear that any changes they make to the sound are beneficial and not detrimental to the sound.

A mastering engineer brings a fresh pair of ears to your project. Everyone involved in your music up to the mixing stage, including the musicians, will be so familiar with the tiniest details of the recording after months of recording and mixing, that they are less able to hear the project as a whole entity, and less able to judge how it sounds at first listen. This fresh perspective, combined with their experience, means that they can hear more easily what final adjustments need to be made to the sound to get the best sound.

The gear in a mastering studio is chosen carefully to be appropriate for working on a whole mix in stereo or 5.1. It is often different from the equipment used to record and mix an album, which is essentially a multi-track process. Whilst it is possible to do the whole process on one workstation using a variety of plugins, most dedicated mastering suites have a collection of digital and analogue processing gear, with high quality A to D and D to A converters to bridge the analogue and digital signal paths.

## The technical process

Mastering happens after your tracks have been mixed, and before they are sent to the pressing plant or duplication house. All mastering begins with the final mixes from the recording stage; CD mastering ends with a CD production master tape, disc or file that is sent to the pressing plant; vinyl mastering ends with a set of lacquers that are sent to the vinyl pressing plant. The mastering session often starts these days with the final mixes on CD, either an audio CD, or as sound files on a CD-Rom. If you are mixing 24 bit, which is always recommended, you will need to burn 24 bit sound files in WAV or AIF format to a CD-Rom, because an audio CD only has a resolution of 16 bits.

The approach to mastering varies from studio to studio and from engineer to engineer, but a typical procedure is as follows.

1. Getting the sound right one track at a time.

   Your mixes are listened to, and if work is needed on the sound, the engineer will use the tools at his disposal to fix any problems with the mix, to get the dynamics and spectral balance (the 'EQ' of a track) right, and to get the level of the mix up to approximately the final level of the CD. This is also the stage where mixes that sound significantly different to each other are treated to minimise the differences between them, to 'pull together' the various mixes. These days there are often tracks recorded and mixed in different studios, sometimes by different people, so this aspect is even more important in that context. The decisions on the sound are not done by any computer or spectral analysis of the music, because there is very little of practical use that can be derived from these – in fact they can be counter-productive by setting you off trying to balance something to make a graph look good at the expense of the music. Experienced mastering engineers use their accurate listening environment, their experience, and most importantly their ears.

When the mix sounds right, it is loaded onto the mastering workstation, the EQs and compressors are reset, and the next track is brought up. It is very rare for the same settings to be used for every song on a project. The settings may be similar, especially if the whole project has come from the same session in the same studio recorded by the same personnel, but each track will sound different and will need its own particular treatment to get the best out of it. If a mix sounds just right as it is, and no extra adjustments need to be made, then it is simply set to the correct level. If a mix sounds particularly bad, the mastering engineer may suggest to the producer or artist that the finished product would benefit from going back a step and adjusting the mix.

2. Compiling.

It is normally the responsibility of the client to decide the running order of the finished CD. The mastering engineer will happily advise, but it is a decision best made before you go to the mastering session. It is easy enough to experiment with different running orders to pick the best one. You can burn a CD with all the tracks, then programme a CD player to play the various potential running orders. Alternatively you can burn a CD of each running order and try them out. If you play gigs regularly you will already have written out dozens of set lists – you can apply that experience to this task. Take your time and pick an order that you are comfortable with. There is no right or wrong, there's just what feels right.

So back to the mastering session: all your tracks sound great and are loaded onto the workstation. The engineer will then compile your tracks into the correct order, paying particular attention to the starts, the fades and/or ends of the tracks, and deciding on the gaps between them.

Setting gaps is a particular art – there is no such thing as a standard gap, and a good engineer will set a gap that simply feels right. For example, a song that ends abruptly will have a longer gap after it than a song that fades out gently, because you will not hear the very end of the faded song so the gap will seem longer than it actually is. Another example is that a fast, loud song followed by a gentler tune will need a long gap because of a change in mood, but two fast songs could feel right with a shorter gap. You can also use the gaps to set the mood of an album: add a second to every gap in an album and the whole thing will feel more laid back and relaxed; remove a second from every gap and you'll get a punchy, almost relentless feel to the whole project.

3. Levelling.

The relative levels of the tracks on a CD should always be set by listening to them. A mastering suite may have two or three different types of meters for reference and for deriving clues about the dynamic range, but the final judge must be the ears of the engineer. The aim is to have the whole CD 'flow' naturally, without the listener having the need to reach for the volume control. It is perfectly acceptable to set gentler songs to be quieter than brash ones, as this reflects the real dynamics of the music when it's played live. Once the relative level of the tracks has been set, the overall level of the CD is decided, and a limiter is applied to trim any peaks that may go over maximum level.

4. Making the master.

This is the stage where everyone sits back and listens to the finished product as the CD production master is made. Traditionally this master would have been a master tape such as a 1630 U-Matic or an Exabyte, but more common these days is a CD master on CD. This final 'listen through' is the opportunity to check back all the work that has been done and to listen to all the decisions that have been made in the context of the whole album. Sometimes small adjustments are made after this listen through, for example half a second's gap added here, a track taken down 1dB there, and another master is made. Often, though, it is the moment of pride and relief for the artist that the CD is now finished and that it actually sounds very good.

## THE COSTS

Naturally, there is a huge range of options when it comes to mastering, each of them aimed at different budgets. If you go to an established mastering facility in London or New York, with a famous mastering engineer that has mastered chart-topping hits, there's almost no limit to the cost, and you can easily spend thousands of pounds. At the other end of the scale, there are people with a workstation, some plug-ins and a decent level of technical knowledge who will master an album for a couple of hundred pounds, perhaps even less. In the middle range, many mastering studios offer budget or fixed price options to artists who are producing their own projects, giving you the advantages of a dedicated mastering facility and engineer without letting the costs run away too much. Allow £300–£600 for an album or £50–£200 for a demo or an EP.

## Mastering at home

If you simply don't have the money to pay someone to master your music, then the process is possible on your home PC or Mac with a few basic programs. On a PC, Nero is a popular CD burning application and Adobe Audition, formerly known as Cool Edit Pro, is a good editor with the ability to use plugins. On a Mac, Toast is the most popular burning software, and Peak is a good basic editing tool.

Follow these guidelines.

- Be gentle with it. If you are using mastering plug-ins like maximisers and finalisers, don't push your music too hard through them. Use gentle settings. Compare before and after.

- Always double-check the effect the processing's had on your music by dropping the level of the processed version to the same perceived level as the original, and comparing A:B. Remember that most things sound better louder, so always compare at similar levels.

- Don't make it sound worse! It sounds obvious, but be aware that multiband compressors can really mess with the sound of a mix. Again, compare before and after at similar levels. Mastering engineers rarely use multiband compressors, and only normally for a particular effect or for a problem with a particular track.

- Set levels by ear.

- Listen to the tracks against each other to set the level. Don't do it by meters, don't allow your computer to 'normalise' it for you. Remember that it's possible to have two tracks that both peak at 0dB full scale on a digital meter, and one could sound much louder than the other because of the way it's been recorded, and because it may have been compressed and/or limited. Trust your ears.

● Check it out on a variety of systems.

● Burn a CD of the finished product. Play it at home, play it in the car, play it on a portable box, listen on headphones. Go back and make changes until you're happy.

● Budget for mastering next time. Before you start your next project, put some money aside for the mastering stage. The end product will sound significantly better for it.

## Conclusion

You have put your soul into writing your music, you've put your heart into arranging it, your sweat and your cash into recording and mixing it. It's only fair to do all of that justice by finishing the process properly.

## INTRODUCTION TO MASTERING (A BIT MORE SCIENCE)

Mastering is the final creative stage of the music production process.

It is the art of crafting a collection of tracks into an album, a CD production master, a vinyl lacquer, or a finished demo. CD mastering begins with the final mixes from the recording stage, and ends with a CD production master tape, disc or file that is sent to the pressing plant.

As mastering engineers we bring specialist skills and equipment to this final stage.

Fresh ears can give a good perspective of an entire project, when everybody else is so focused in on the detail that they have lost sight of the overall context. We create balanced and accurate listening environments where we can hear, and compensate for, any anomalies in the recording process.

Mastering engineers are specialists. We don't claim to be experts at recording or mixing, because we have spent most of our careers mastering. For similar reasons, most recording engineers and producers prefer to pass their work on to a mastering engineer for the final stage.

## The listening environment

The first thing a mastering engineer needs is a great sounding room. In that room he will put some very good speakers.

Acoustic treatment and high-quality monitoring are crucial to a good mastering suite. With a balanced, accurate listening environment, it is possible to hear exactly how a recording sounds, and make judgements based on those observations. Mastering engineers probably spend more time, energy, money, sweat and tears on acoustics and monitoring than on any other aspect of a mastering facility.

## D to A & A to D converters

Most high-end mastering engineers like to use good analogue equipment for a lot of the sound processing that they do. High calibre analogue to digital and digital to analogue converters are therefore essential to ensure that the conversion between the analogue and digital domains is as accurate and real as possible. Listening tests prove time and again that there can be a huge difference in quality between different converters, and so as mastering engineers we choose our converters very carefully and select only the best.

## Compression

Applying compression reduces the dynamic range of the signal being processed.

This involves making louder sounds quieter, and conversely, once you have applied a make-up gain, making quieter sounds louder.

Applying compression to an entire mix is very different to compressing individual instruments, as you might during the recording process. When mixing, for example, you might compress a lead vocal heavily to make sure that it is at a constant level and always cuts through the mix. During the mastering process, however, we are applying a compressor to the whole mix: some sounds will be triggering the compressor, but all sounds will be affected by it.

Used clumsily, compression can flatten, distort, muddy and strangle your music.

Used judiciously, compression can add punch, clarity, drive and feeling to your music.

## Equalisation

Usually called EQ, equalisation applies gain to a certain frequency while leaving others unchanged.

We use EQs to change the spectral balance of the music, in other words, to boost or cut various low, mid and high frequency ranges.

This can be used for a number of effects.

- To compensate for anomalies in the listening environment it was mixed in.

- To bring clarity to vocals, guitars, snare, horns and other mid-range instruments.

- To clear up a muddy bass, to add punch to a kick drum, to sparkle the cymbals.

- To make all the tracks in a project sound balanced next to each other.

Once again, EQ used badly can destroy, EQ used judiciously can transform.

## Noise reduction

The process of tackling unwanted noises happens in the digital domain. These noises might be clicks, crackles, hiss, buzz or pops. Each particular noise has a different process that attempts to reduce the effect of the noise without too much of a detrimental effect to the music.

It is possible to eliminate certain noises completely, such as a light crackle or sharp high clicks, by reconstructing the sound very accurately and unnoticeably to the ear. Hiss and buzz, however, are often spread more broadly across the audio spectrum. Care must be taken not to create artefacts in the music as a result of removing unwanted noise.

The best noise reduction processor in the world is the most common – the human brain. You'll notice that when you listen to music on vinyl, you only notice the noise and crackles for about half a minute, thereafter your brain simply doesn't listen to them. The same happens when watching an old film – it's not long before the drama takes over and you forget all about the old grainy print.

Brian Eno once drew an analogy between tape hiss and the texture of canvas. Canvas paintings, he said, have a look and a feel that are a direct result of the medium they're painted on, and that's part of their character. The same applies to a tape recording, he claimed, which will give music a unique sound defined by the limits of the medium onto which it is recorded. This becomes part of the character of the recording.

## Level control

Levelling is one of the most powerful and often overlooked tools in a mastering engineer's arsenal.

Setting the relative levels or volumes of each track is arguably the mastering engineer's most important job. An album must have a level, or volume, balance – with quieter songs sitting naturally alongside louder songs. An album should have dynamics too. An album should play through sounding even, without the need to adjust the volume.

The mastering engineer's ears must be the final judge of the loudness of a track.

We will use different meters for reference, all with different meter ballistics and meter rules.

All these will help, but the final judgement must be that of our ears.

Never believe a digital tool that claims to 'normalise' tracks to the same level. Trust only your ears.

## Limiting

A limiter is used to reduce the level of the highest peaks in an audio signal. We use limiters to raise the perceived level of sound without creating over levels. Once we have balanced the relative levels of your tracks, we will use a limiter to raise the loudness of the music to the optimum overall level.

Once again, delicacy is required to achieve the required level without causing distortion.

See On the Loudness Wars later in this chapter for further discussion of levels and limiting.

## PQing

This process is where the track start and end times are set for a CD. A CD player uses this information to skip to the start of any track. These start and end 'indexes' are called PQ points.

Often, these marks are obvious: when there is silence between tracks, there is a distinct start and end time for each track. In this example, PQ points can often be placed automatically.

Sometimes there are no gaps in the audio on an album, for example, a live album will have applause and audience noise; a concept album may have additional ambient material between tracks. In these cases, PQ points must be set at the most natural place for a track to start. In these cases also, the end point of one track will be the same as the start point for the next track.

## Making the master

Once all the work is complete, we will then create the CD production master. This is what is used by the pressing plant to replicate the finished CDs. The CD master is usually played off the mastering workstation in real time. This is the point where we listen through to check that the project plays well as a complete work.

A CD production master can come in many forms. These are the ones used by Masteringworld.

### Exabyte tape

This is an 8mm data tape, on which is stored a DDP image (direct to disc protocol) and extra files with PQ information. This is the format preferred by most factories.

### CD master data on a CD-Rom

Exactly the same DDP data as the Exabyte can be burned to a data CD on a computer's CD-Rom drive. This is the most reliable way for a CD master to be delivered online. Download the DDP set of files, burn them to CD-Rom as data, and hand the disc to your replicator.

### FTP direct to the factory

Again, this is the same DDP data, and it can be delivered online direct to the factory. Advise the mastering engineer which factory will be pressing your CDs and he will transfer your CD master data to them.

## Audio CD

Pressing plants and duplicators will also accept audio CDs for replicating, subject to conditions. It must have been burnt as a disc-at-once session and must also have been finalised. The CD master can be delivered to you as a disc image that can then be burned to a CD. Professional mastering workstations create images in either DDP or .jam formats. Make sure you have software that can burn a .jam image, for example Toast with Jam.

# On the loudness wars

To keep up with demand for CDs to be louder, louder, and louder again, mastering engineers have been relying more and more on compressors and limiters to coax the loudest levels out of a given format. In the days of vinyl cutting, the pressure was to get the loudest 'cut' onto the vinyl master. These days, the same competition for loudness is happening to the CD format.

Any digital format has a finite limit to the loudness of a signal recorded onto it, defined by the number of bits – in the case of a CD, 16 bits per word. In order to make a CD sound louder, the music must be pushed closer and closer to that maximum level, using compressors and limiters. Before compression or limiting, a piece of music may have dynamics – quiet parts, medium parts, loud parts and very loud parts. The louder you want a CD to be, the more you must take away from those dynamics. What is often left at the end of this process is all the elements of the music forced to be as loud as is possible. Whilst this can make a track sound punchy, hard and powerful, it can also make the music fatiguing to the human ear, which misses the variety of dynamics.

Of course, if loudness is the most important factor to you, a good mastering engineer will use all the tricks he knows to put the maximum boost into your music. Please consider, however, the advantages of leaving some dynamic range in your finished CDs. Your music will sound more natural, more expressive and more real.

## RECORDING IN HOME STUDIOS

This is where investing in a home studio comes into its own. A good make of PC or laptop costs very little and there are always computer companies fighting with each other over getting you to buy their product. The upside is that you win each time. Bands should start thinking like collectives and banding together to get the gear they all need to make high quality digital recordings. For £1,000 you can spend £500 on the computer, which leaves the other five on the music software of your choice. Most digital software works much the same as another. So the choice comes down to personal preference and what feels right for you. The best way to find this out is to get into your local music emporium and have a play around. You will also be able to download demo versions of the software to try out and I would recommend you try them all. The internet is loaded with reviews on every piece of software out there and there is no shortage of experts voicing their opinions on what rocks and what doesn't.

However, you should understand that recording music is a technical subject that requires time, patience, learning and vast amounts of practice. The music software itself has educational courses that can take a few months to get through.

### Getting set up

My weapon of choice would be Pro Tools Mbox 2. The Mbox is the interface you record though onto the computer and the software is the world class Pro Tools. It's inexpensive, highly professional, and great to work with. You can and will record music on this rig that The Beatles back in the 60s would have killed for. It's really as simple as getting some decent mics, plugging everything in, arming the track and playing the chords. There are some great training books and DVDs in most shops. Of course it will take a few months to get your head around the software, but the results will be worth it.

There are a few things to consider and understand. When setting up a home studio it's best to have a room dedicated solely to recording. Most of you will probably still be at home or at college and even then with some thought you can start up in a clutter-free environment. The checklist of what you will need is:

- a computer

- a soundcard

- monitoring speakers

- software (some come with a digital interface like Pro Tools).

Choosing manufacturers

Most PC manufacturers are cut-throat in selling you their products. One company is as good as another.

- Dell (**www.dell.co.uk**) make great PCs, their products are strong, reliable and sturdy. They may not be the best looking computers out there but they do look after you when it comes to customer service.

- PC World (**www.pcworld.co.uk**) sell computers from most manufacturers and you get the chance to go and road test what you are after. I would always go for a laptop. It makes life easier, takes up less space and they are now as powerful as their desktop big brothers.

- Apple (**www.apple.com/uk**) for some of you will be the only choice and whilst their top end range is expensive you can get Macs as cheap as any PC.

Again, the Mac laptops are fantastic pieces of kit. I have to say that I never found them any more or less reliable than the PC as they are prone to crashing like any computer is, but it will come down to your own preference. Don't get into the mindset that one is better than the other. I use both PCs and Macs for different purposes and really hate those holier-than-thou merchants proclaiming which platform is best. Ultimately the platform you choose will be dependent on your own needs. So don't be swayed by the converted, do the research and make up your own minds.

## Sound cards

Sound cards are needed for laptops and will be an extra expense, but this should still fit into a budget of £1,000 for all you need. Desktops come with blistering power and sound cards already installed. Creative labs sounds cards are standard but again it's down to your own needs. Digital is digital so what would spin it for me is the number of input/output plugs a sound card has. www.creativelabs.com will contain everything you need to know about their products. For the laptop a sound card will cost around £80 for an audigy. It fits into an expansion slot on the side of the laptop where you will hardly notice it. The higher range Apple laptops come with a pre-installed sound card.

## Software

The software option again is down to user preference. I would always go into a shop and get a feel for the different programs available. You can download trial versions to see how you get on and this is recommended. I've tried most digital software and found them all to be excellent. All of them perform the same jobs and that's to get you recording digitally. The only difference is the learning curve everyone faces. These programs are professional platforms and the end product will solely depend on how proficient you become. The more time and energy you spend learning the better the recordings are going to be. There are many books and educational DVDs along with courses on these programs for you to learn from. So, it's just down to you.

Some ideas for software...

### Reason

www.propellerheads.se

Reason is a fully functional self-contained musical software studio. Containing its own sequencer Reason is an amalgam of mixers, synths and samplers. The Prodigy use Reason to record albums and that in itself is a huge endorsement. If you want to know what Reason is capable of, listen to the latest Prodigy album. Available on both PC and Mac.

## Cubase

www.steinberg.net

Cubase SX/SL is probably the most used home recording software. Containing both a MIDI and audio sequencer it provides the user with the means to record, edit, play back and mix both MIDI and audio recordings.

## Logic Audio

www.apple.com/logicpro

A sole-based Mac platform MIDI audio package. Very powerful with an almost unlimited amount of flexibility. Rammstein use Logic, that's not to say you may be able to get as hard a sound or degree of supersonic athletics when you start to learn it, but it gives you an idea of what it is capable of.

## Sonar

www.cakewalk.com

Sonar have made massive advances since the days of cakewalk, with several editions from Producer to full recording systems. Available for PC only Sonar runs off 64 bit technology as well as 32 bit. I know people who swear by Sonar because of the vast array of tools at its disposal. ACID style audio and MIDI loops along with mastering software make Sonar a great all round choice.

## Pro Tools

www.digidesign.com

Pro Tools is the industry standard and thanks to Pro Tools LE along with the M Box you can now have this excellent program banging out your CD. The biggest selling point of Pro Tools is the elegance of the software interface. This doesn't mean it's simple but it is intuitive to get to grips with. With a range of audio effects available it has become many bands' new weapon of choice in the recording arena.

This was really only to give you a basic idea of what is available to you. The power each of these programs has is unique to the times you live in. However, like most creative areas, it will always come down to the individual. One book I would recommend on the subject of home based recording is *The Illustrated Home Recording Handbook* available from www.flametreepublishing.com which will get you started and go into depth on all the areas you will need to cover.

## A VOICE FROM THE MUSIC INDUSTRY

Lastly for this section I spoke to Michael Laskow from the music industry website **www.taxi.com** about his thoughts on the future of artists and record labels. For anyone who doesn't know the Taxi website it is a great independent A&R service for unsigned bands/artists that can place you directly into the hands of labels, publishers or even TV companies. It has a great section on music industry advice that includes articles from songwriting, to touring, A&R and anything else you can think of related to the music industry. If you are not a member you should get over there and sign up as the site and the information contained on it will help you out immensely. I have actually referenced some of the articles during the research for this book from it. I think Michael gives a great insight.

### How do you see the recording industry developing in the future?

Obviously, with the advent of all the great home recording gear that's out there now, it's possible for everybody and anybody to make great sound recordings. The internet makes it possible for the artists and bands to take their music direct to the consumer. Given that, one might think that record companies will quickly become unnecessary, but that puts the burden on marketing the music on the shoulders of the bands and artists. My experience has been that most creative people don't really want to accept that responsibility, nor do they often want to do the hard work of learning how to market their music. So, in the end, while they're able to make a great recording, it's often a recording that will never reach a mass audience.

A lot of people think that MySpace and YouTube are replacements for old-school record companies, but with 3 million artists and bands on MySpace alone, the question is 'what can I do to stand out and compete with the other 2,999,999 bands that are on MySpace?' It sounds like there's a great opportunity for somebody to write the book to solve that problem, but then all 3,000,000 bands will read it and be back on a level playing field with nobody coming up the winner.

### Do bands have a realistic chance of creating a career for themselves using digital technology and the internet?

I think that the days of the giant mega-hit may be near an end. So, if you consider $50,000–100,000 a year a reasonable living wage, then I think the answer is yes. I think that we'll see thousands of bands making a living wage instead of a dozen making mega dollars. I like to call that 'the musician middle-class'. But I think that we'll see that the bands that can make that $50–100K year after year are the same hardworking people that would build a following, do a lot of touring and sell thousands of CDs out of the trunks of their cars after shows in the old record business. In other words, the people who would have been successful in the old-school model will most likely take that same work ethic and use that to create success in the new direct to consumer model.

# The CD Pressing

There are many CD and DVD media pressing companies throughout the UK. Most deliver the goods for around the same price, depending obviously on the specific requirements. A regular 1,000 CD run with jewel cases, barcode, four pages and delivery costs in the region of £800. Yes, there will always be those companies who will either match others or who will undercut, but I think it's better to go with those who respond to your initial enquiry with that extra touch.

## FINDING A COMPANY

I researched ten companies across the UK and most were very competitive with each other. Some of the London-based companies were slightly arrogant in that a small band were really not that important (London sort your act out), which turned me off from going any further with them. I was impressed with the pressing companies in smaller towns but for sheer easiness and going that bit further www.a1cds.co.uk came out on top. A1cds had a question and answer section along with other relevant info any young band may need to understand the process of getting CDs pressed. This makes life easier for everyone, cuts down the research time and makes you want to use their company. So, **www.a1cds.co.uk** is officially endorsed by The Rock and Roll Times for doing what all companies should, looking after the bands, the bread and butter...

## What to look for

- Your initial enquiry will be along the lines of how much for a certain amount of CDs. Most companies will have an online submission quote form. The final cost to you depends on your requirements. The more you want from the CD the more it will cost. The first choice is the actual amount of CDs. Most bands will go for a start run of 1,000 CDs.

- The next stage is how many colours you want on the body of the CD itself. If you have elaborate artwork then it would require more colours than just plain old writing on a silver CD.

- Then you have a choice when it comes to the booklet. Artwork, pics and lyrics along with thanking everyone and their granny goes into this part and again you choose between either two to 12 pages in full colour or one page in colour and one in black and white.

- The inlay tray again is either colour or black and white, or both, and ranges from no inlay tray to four pages.

The packaging choices are numerous and I would go with what you like most about CDs yourself. Packaging and presentation goes a long way and as it could be your debut album don't scrimp on doing the best job. You can either choose the standard jewel case, maxi case or wallet, plastic wallet, full colour card wallet or a nice white envelope style. By this point the cost is dependent on all requirements so far. But this is your release out to the world: make sure you adhere to the budget you have, but still make sure you make it stylish.

Most companies have free delivery and will need the source files of the music so they can turn it into the glass master they need to press your CD. All the websites I looked at did state what requirements they needed from the band, so take your time and make sure you send everything you need to. Anything you are still not sure about, simply call them up for a chat. With most music recorded on digital media, pressing companies have the technology to turn digital files into glass masters.

## GETTING A BARCODE

The next stage is selling your CD and for this you will need a barcode. Pressing companies used to be able to supply barcodes free of charge, but then the Barcode Association clamped down and advised pressing companies they could no longer supply barcodes for independent projects. So you now have to go and do it for yourselves. You can easily issue your own EAN 13 digit barcodes: visit the GS1UK website http://www.gs1uk.org/home.asp and make the arrangements to become a member. It will cost about £98 to join and around £98 for a year's membership. However, there is a way around you having to fork out an extra 200 quid for this privilege and that's joining iTunes or Cdbaby. That will all be covered in the next chapter. I'm not one for spending money where it isn't needed and I think with the Barcode Association clamping down it has actually worked out in the bands' favour. The next chapter explains all.

It's worth mentioning that should you be issued with a barcode then any pressing company worth their salt will still apply the image or number to the CD artwork free of charge.

### About the barcode

The UK uses EAN 13 digit barcodes. Your barcode will have a unique number that is assigned to your product only. This number will allow you to place your product for sale in any UK resale outlet that requires barcoded products.

Radio stations use barcodes to help track and log plays of particular tracks for royalty collection. And this obviously helps when it comes to chart positioning. Well, you still want your album in the charts, don't you?

### Adding the barcode to your artwork

The pressing company will either supply you or your designer with a barcode image to use or place it on your artwork for you.

The barcode should be on the (K) layer of your CMYK design (black) and for accurate scanning should have a white background. Keeping it to one colour (black) will result in a crisp, sharp print that will enable scanners to easily read the code.

That's the gist of this one. The next chapter is a lot more fun. It's where you learn how to get your music out into the world.

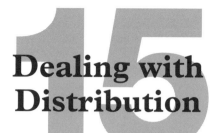

# Dealing with Distribution

Commandment Seven

An unsigned band seeking distribution to get their CD into the shops are going to find it very tough, if not impossible. That's because most distributors deal solely with record labels and not bands directly. Whilst there are a few bands that can get a distribution deal without a label, they are few and far between. So, this is really an area were you will need a record deal in order to get your CD into the shops. However, we won't be just looking at physical distribution. The digital area will be talked about and I think that will make you happier. I would never give you a negative without a positive.

## WHAT DISTRIBUTORS DO – AND DON'T DO

Let's look at the role of a distributor so you understand what they do when it comes to setting up your own record label. Oh yes, you will be setting up one of those babies too!

Distribution companies are in business to get physical CDs and DVDs into shops. Space is always at a premium and with many independent record shops having gone out of business most towns will have either a HMV or Virgin store as the place to get your new release. Of course there are other retail shops that will stock products too, but when digital technology entered the marketplace all your cool indies disappeared. Many think tanks declare the death of physical CDs due to the kids downloading illegally, but I never seem to read about the vast processing plants in Asia churning out illegal CDs or DVDs that end up being sold at car boot sales or over the internet. The men in suits failed to realise that times were changing and instead of embracing a new kind of business model and working out new ways to bring better value to physical releases they went after the kids.

The problem is that you have an industry that is essentially lead by the consumer, but is managed by old farts. They don't have any visionaries that tell the board members that the new generation of music buyer has grown up with computers and has gotten used to getting things when they want. Life has sped up faster than we can cope with and the days where anyone really wants to wait six months to hear a new song are over. Why wait when you can download it in minutes now? That's an inherent problem the entire music industry is facing. A total sea change in how it conducts its business.

The answers won't be found in this book, but going after 13-year-olds isn't the answer. I'm not denying there isn't a problem, but until the industry gets its house in order you will continue to read about falling sales and how badly digital download is affecting it. Digital distribution is simply the main platform we will all use in the future. Whichever way you analyse it, in the future when the oil runs out and we have consumed the planet's resources (CD packaging is made from oil) or we have no more trees left (for your lovely covers), the only option will be the digital platform.

## The distributor's job

A distributor's job is to get a new release into the record shop. Lack of space in an overcrowded market makes this job harder and harder, which eventually trickles down to the record labels vying for less real estate when it comes to having any new product placed.

Like the rest of the industry distribution companies can either be the huge corporations or a small, specialist indie. Commission is taken on each record sold placed by a distributor. They don't buy records, they place them. Should they not succeed in placing those records or those records failing to sell then they get returned to you, with all charges being incurred by you. The average signing period to a distribution deal is around two years, but it will vary with specific opt-out clauses on both sides should things not work out to expectations. If you plan on creating a professional record label then you will need a distribution deal. Whilst you may be able to persuade your local HMV to stock a few CDs you won't be able to do that around the entire country. **Signing a distribution deal is one of the fundamental elements you will need in place before you storm the world.**

# THE RIGHT DISTRIBUTOR

Large-scale distributors will tend to focus on all genres, but there are some that will specialise, whether it's dance or hip hop for instance. You will need to research which one is suitable for you. Whichever kind of genre you are will give you an idea of which distributor you should talk to. A distributor that specialises in your genre of music will have the right contacts and know which shops will be receptive to a new release and particular style of music. When you go online to check out distribution websites they will list the styles of music they sign. So use your commonsense. Don't be sending a metal release to a dance specialist, ok!

When you are a small-scale operation distributors will get copies of your release into the smaller shops around the country. The point of this is to see if your music is working and when the CDs start to fly out of the shops you will then be taken into the larger arena of the mega stores and placed in every town. This may take some time, but distributors know their future is in selecting the right labels to build a relationship with, along with developing them.

## Label management

The distribution label structure is more or less the same as any industry organisation. The label management team are like the A&R guys. These will be the people you initially approach. They decide which labels to take on and will work with that label, handling the development during the contract term. So, when it's time to approach a distributor ask for the label management when you call or email them.

## Sales department

The sales department's job is to get the stock into the shops. They will also provide labels with advice and guidance on marketing and promotional activities within the shops. Mostly this will cost money and when you first enter a shop all those lovely CDs or DVDs you encounter are there because they have paid a higher premium to be displayed. You see, psychological testing has determined that you as a consumer will forget what you've gone into the shop for in the first place, so it's better to pay a stack load more money to hit you over the head when you enter the shop. Listening post previews and any PR activity you see such as posters and flyers will cost extra money too.

Everything you see in a record shop is rented space and the ones who ultimately pay for it all are the artists. However, this kind of activity is reserved for the big guns. The big labels with the expenditure. The sales team will advise you on what level you should hit and it will always be limited to the budget you have.

## The music

Distributors, like everyone else in the industry, will want to see you grow and develop. They will have established that you are worth the time and investment when it comes to the music you have or will sign, develop and A&R in the future. As well as gauging how good you are, it means they can plan the release dates to keep you in the limelight and build your reputation. This is because they will develop a plan over a set period of time to build your profile and keep your music in the public ears and eye. Anyway, you are not doing this part time. You're doing this because it's the sole reason for you being on the planet. So, with the music you have recorded and the passion you will display, along with some nice hits, you will have already given yourself a good foundation to be taken seriously.

## Promotion

The distribution stage is normally the last stage of the plan. It's when the product gets into the public domain. Don't approach a distributor with a fistful of CD-Rs. They won't tend to take you seriously. So that means getting a certain amount of CDs pressed. Now, you already know how to do that because you read the CD pressing chapter right? And hopefully you are getting large amounts of hits from the songs already available on your website, and now the kids are pouring into your shows and the music journos are loving your single. It's time to put together a **press and promotional plan.** That will show the distributor how serious and committed you are and give them something to work with. It will make them excited to know that you have put the work in on the level required to get the imagination of the public focused on you. If you can show you are getting hits, or radio play, and you can email press cuttings from the great reviews you are getting, then you will be in a lot more of an attractive position than just calling to ask for a deal.

Distribution deals are exclusive. You will be signed to one distributor per contract and term. Again, it would be silly to define the ins and outs of a contract here as things are changing and you all know by now to get legal advice, etc before you commit. You will be advised to do so by a distributor anyway. Unless of course they are a scam merchant and I do know there are a few out there which some bands still sign to. However, the big guns are very professional so don't get too paranoid.

## THE DISTRIBUTOR'S VIEW

I asked Luke Selby from Vital Distribution some questions from his perspective as a distributor.

### What is the distributor's role in the music industry?

The role can vary from company to company. Essentially a distributor has traditionally been the penultimate link in the production process of recorded music (if the final link is between shop and record buying fan). That sounds very 'dry' but it encompasses getting the music physically distributed around the world. So as well as selling and physically shipping the product, a distributor is also involved in making sure the artist's music is profiled in store and advises the label on price, packaging, etc. Increasingly distributors are branching out to offer a wider range of services and many now get involved in promotion, manufacturing, and even marketing for a label.

### What do distributors look for in bands?

Distributors generally represent an entire label, often exclusively. As the size and type of independent distributor varies greatly, so does what they're looking for. The bottom line is, of course, financial. Most distribution works off a fee on the selling price so they will want to work with labels with a potential to sell. In addition a great partnership will see a label and a distributor developing their business together, so a label needs to have foresight, plans for the future and the ambition to grow and evolve. An exciting release schedule and solid roster is a must for the modern distributor in almost all instances.

### How should a band approach a distributor?

Again as a general rule (excepting very established artists) it's labels that will make an approach. As above in order to arrange and then hold a productive meeting a label will need to have a good package put together of previously released music, or if a new label a good-looking release schedule of a few releases. Moreover, in addition to finding the right distributor for the size and type of your label, an understanding of the mechanics of the industry, and a firm idea of how the label is going to market promote and develop its artists, will help gain interest for a distributor. If a label can demonstrate it has the desire and ability to stimulate demand for its product then it's already becoming a 'good catch' for interested distributors.

### Does a band need a record deal to be signed to a distributor?

More often than not, yes. In the case of a large artist, often leaving a successful record deal, there are increasing examples of artists in the modern market being in a position to release their own music on their own 'label'. This requires a great team around the artist and of course a good level of funding.

### How long does a distribution deal last for?

This can wholly depend, though often they are two or three years in the independent sector.

### What would you as a distributor advise bands to do?

To get their career going. Promote themselves everywhere they can, use the amazing resource that the internet has become to get your music heard and your profile out there: many things now in the technological age we live in will cost you much less money than a similar level of awareness-raising would have cost even five years ago. Get out there and play wherever you can, meet fellow musicians, meet industry professionals, hustle, learn as much as you can. Knowledge is your biggest tool and you can get it mostly for free. Speak to people with experience, soak up information from everywhere, have belief, be patient, get some good legal advice before you sign anything. And don't give up!

*Has physical distribution been affect by digital sales?*

Yes, definitely. Physical sales have been dropping but still make up the vast majority of album sales, but the market is changing fast.

The platform most of you will want to focus on for now is the digital arena. You will see a lot more activity far sooner getting your music onto the net and selling CDs as downloads or as physical CDs via your website.

## DIGITAL DISTRIBUTION

Once again I'm a fan of making life easy for myself.

## Awal

Whilst researching how a band/artist can get their music placed in iTunes I came across www.awal.co.uk who are the very people you need to go and talk to. Based in the UK their website is concise and straight to the point with any question you would care to know about being asked. Awal's job is to get your music placed on iTunes. They have a simple two-page contract downloadable from their website that requires you to supply two CDs with song and album information along with artwork. For every £0.79 paid per download of one of your songs Awal take 15 per cent commission. As an example, if Apple pay Awal the dealer price of 47p, Awal collect 15 per cent (7.05p), leaving you the band with 39.95p per download. This is around 50 per cent. The accounts are quarterly.

That's your first choice. You now have a second and I have to tell you straight away you cannot sign up to both of these companies. It's one or the other. Now you can have a look at what these guys do and make up your own minds…

## CD Baby

Another great service from a company is the one CD Baby offers you. An American-based company, which means the financial breakdown here is $US dollars. CD Baby is an online record store that sells CDs by independent musicians. Since its founding in 1997 the company has helped over 150,000 artists sell over $40 million in physical CDs, digital downloads, and live sales. A simple $35 (£20) setup will get your music selling worldwide on CD Baby.com, Apple iTunes, Yahoo Music, Best Buy, Rhapsody, Napster, MSN Music and more. Your CD will then be available to over 2,400 traditional retail CD stores in the USA. You get paid full retail price for these sales.

Head to www.cdbaby.com and read through the information. See if it's for you then proceed to the submissions page. As always be clear you are sure of everything you read and take your time. A web page dedicated to selling your CD will be created and includes sound clips, links back to your own website, reviews, along with everything a band profile page needs to tell the world who you are and how they can buy your music. You are given a webpage that is linked from your site to the www.cdbaby.com/bandname page so when any one wants to buy your music direct they can do so.

The company boasts of over 150,000 hits a day from people who are looking for new independent CDs to buy. That's a good hit rate if a lot of those people actually buy the product. You set your selling price at whatever price you think is appropriate, but it's worth talking to the company to discuss what is realistic, along with researching what other bands are selling their CDs for too. For the physical sales that are sold in the shops they will take $4 (retail) per CD sold. That works out at around £2, which if you sell enough CDs in any given shop is not bad at all. (At the time of writing the good old British pound is slaying the bad old Yankee dollar.) For digital distribution and live sales, they take a flat nine per cent cut, leaving the artist with 91 per cent.

Royalty payments are discussed on the site but it looks like standard practice of quarterly accounting. You can cancel at any time without any charges being issued. And as they are a distributor they will hold no rights to your music or CD. Their job is to simply (ha!) get your music into the shops and make it available online.

## Choosing your digital distributor

When it comes to choosing a digital distributor you can only sign to one company in order to get your music onto iTunes or other digital platforms. What's attractive about CD Baby is that they also provide barcodes for you to sell your album in shops for £10, which is a massive reduction on the cost the Barcode Association would have you pay (£200). This makes life a shed-load easier for you as the company will place your CD amongst the 2,400 stores it has deals with in the US. That's not to say your CD will be available in every one of those 2,400 US CD shops, but even if you get your music in a few of those shops and sell out you are on your way to building your US profile. There is a lot more this company offers that you may be interested in, but if I go any further I will end up sounding like their PR guy.

As time marches on there will be other companies popping up with this kind of service. It takes the hassle from the bands having to do it for themselves when it comes to financial transactions, but always read the small print and, if you can, get your friendly local spider, sorry solicitor, to check out the small print.

# Press Ganged

*viii*

**Every day is thy rock n' roll Sabbath**

Commandment Eight

A band should consider themselves like the Revolutionary Warfare Wing of the SAS. Each person in the team is trained to a high standard in a particular field. This field is the press. If none of you have any journalistic experience then it's time to recruit someone. If you are at university then you should know someone studying media or journalism who can cut their teeth in doing the press for the band. Recruit a fanzine writer or find someone who is busting to break into music journalism. There are always more people trained or in training for this role than there are jobs available. It's better to gain experience working for a band than it is getting job rejections. The point I'm making is use your savvy, be streetwise, you are bound to come into contact with someone you can create a symbiotic relationship with. And if anyone in the band is handy with words then do it for yourselves. All you need is a computer, a scanner and printer.

## CREATIVE PUBLICITY

The software required is Microsoft Word, which comes with all PCs, and if you can, some desktop publishing software depending on how elaborate things become. This will make it easy and cheap to produce a publicity pack. Most software packages will come with formatted templates, and a variety of free and easy designs enabling you to produce business cards, flyers and biographies.

Be creative and stay away from normal-looking styles. Incorporate colours and cool designs from artwork the band already has designed. However, try not to go too over the top, the presentation needs to be cool but readable. In this day and age you really don't need to go to a publishing company to do all the design work. Do as much work in-house as possible. This keeps all the costs down.

## YOUR PUBLICITY PACK

Once you have established who is in charge of press and publicity the next step is creating the publicity pack. This is where you can go to town, but make sure it is tasteful because the more information a magazine or newspaper has the better the story they can get from it. Include any weird or funny stories, along with interesting ones of course surrounding the band. As this is rock and roll you as a band/artist are bound to have some events surrounding the band that make interesting reading. A journalist will always be more eager to place a news story if they have something to stick their teeth into. Local press are always looking for that local band angle. If you are getting record company interest, mention it. If you have your video played on TV, mention it. If you have a head-banging budgie as a band mascot, again, you know what to do.

Here's what you will need for your publicity pack in no particular order.

## Photograph

A press pack should contain photographs of the band. You will all have a mobile phone that will take pictures if you cannot get hold of a good quality camera. The pixilation on phones can be very good and using Photoshop you can get good quality shots of the band. So, there is really no excuse to not have any photos. Try not to make the pose too clichéd, but in this day and age it's difficult to get a good band pic that hasn't already been done. Professionally taken photos are expensive and I would advise you to buy a good camera and get to use it rather than pay out hundreds of pounds on something you would only really use a few times. Live shots of the band playing gigs are good, as are staged shots in your home town. It goes without saying that any photos should be recent ones.

People like to see what bands look like. Most bands will have an image so make sure this is consistent with your music. A band's image is a style statement and must go hand in hand with your style of music. You are making a statement not only on music but in fashion too, whether it's obvious or not.

Always keep in mind that photographs are also used for reprinting in newspapers and magazines, so make sure your prints aren't too dark or grainy. If you supply photos separately then make sure the pic includes your band name and contact information at the bottom (phone number, mailing address, email address and website URL).

## Copy of your album

As this is for press purposes it's worth including your entire album as you do want to get it reviewed in a magazine or newspaper and of course fanzines. If it's to book gigs then perhaps a selection of four of your best songs is better. A lot of A&R may say they only need four songs, but you know what, it's easy to switch the CD off after they have made their minds up. I would always advocate sending a full album out. This shows your intentions and the fact that you are playing by your own rules means you have not compromised. Don't believe the hype as the new cliché goes.

The only point I would make here is cost. Always try to keep costs down because if it takes all of your money to send your CDs to places, people or magazines for it to just sit on a desk then it will be a waste. Even top bands have this problem. However, if you are about to embark on a 30-date tour then calling the local press for a chat to see how receptive they are is worth it. There is a certain amount of collateral damage to be had when you are in this period of the campaign so make sure you keep tabs on who has the CD and always place a 'For promotional purposes only' sticker on all press-related CDs.

## Act or band biography and contact number

Keep the bio short so it fills one side of A4 paper. Stick to the facts. The bio should contain information on who the members are, what instruments they play and any interesting background info concerning the band. If you want to be really creative an A5 piece of paper folded in two turns it into a mini booklet. The front page should contain the band's logo with a small pic underneath. Page two contains the bio, leaving page three with any funny or interesting stories and page four with upcoming gig info.

A biography (or bio) should be kept short and sweet. There will come a time when you can write the full history of the band. But for now if there's a unique story about how your band formed or about the various members in your group, include it. This gives writers at newspapers and magazines a special twist or hook when writing about your band. If you have any cool quotes or reviews, include them here as well but don't over do it. Including 15 quotes from people no one has ever heard off is pointless and boring. For your reference check out other bands' bios on the web and see what their approach is. If you have any accomplishments they are important to list in your bio, for example if you have any endorsements from guitar or drum companies. Maybe you have sold out the first batch of 1,000 CDs, or your current video is blazing all over the internet and TV.

## Posters

Posters are a great link to the fans to keep as souvenirs. It's worthwhile sending some posters ahead of time to any venue with a big pic of the band on front. The fans will take these down and get you to sign them and it should always be encouraged.

## Flyers

I've never thought flyers did much good. It may be ok to have money-off flyers for some fans to hand into the venue upon entry, but as far as a tool for promotion it mostly doesn't work. Before you enter any gig people are always handing out flyers and how many are actually used? Most end up on the floor wasting money and far too many trees. I think it's much better to have a mailing list sheet to grab emails, etc. My basic point will always come down to finance and you should invest any limited money you have into something much more worthwhile.

## Gig dates

Gig dates can be emailed when booked to fans, agents, venues, etc to keep everyone updated.

## Press clippings

Any reviews from magazines, fanzines or anything from a music website that make you look good should be placed together in a press clippings folder.

As venues, agents, promoters, managers, record labels and publishers receive stacks of unsolicited material daily it's really best to only send a press pack to them after it has been requested. The likelihood is that it will otherwise end up in the bin. Again, it's a cost issue and you do not want any wastage. Always be professional.

## Cover letter

The cover letter should be the introduction to the band. Thank whoever you have sent the press pack to or whoever requested it and make sure you state the band name, with all relevant contact info, name, tel numbers and website. Be patient for the response and place a call a week or so later to see the state of play. Should you get no response after a few tries then move on, they will not be interested. However, most professional companies will get back to you with a yes or no.

In the age of digital media and fast-food timing make sure your website contains all the info the press pack has, along with mp3 and a section for press and media. Most people will not wait around for packages and would rather access who you are immediately. One day the need to send out hard copy press packs will cease so start thinking this way. It will save time, money and trees. Anyone needing pics of the band will ask you to send it via a J-peg, etc and now you get the point.

## THE ELECTRONIC PRESS KIT (EPK)

The electronic press kit is where it's all heading. This will be a video shot to a song that introduces the band like a trailer to a movie. It's like a grand opening and when done properly it can be very effective and exciting. It's the digital age so make use of it.

Your electronic press kit is essentially a video segment consisting of a combination of music video clips, gig performances, rehearsal performances, band interviews and snap shots of the band's life. This can be placed on the website or used in a DVD or VCD to promote the band to journalists, venues, managers and record labels, etc. Effective, visually fantastic and a complete must to get organised. Study as many bands who have these as you can before plotting what your EPK should say, do and show before you do yours. Research is key to understanding what makes a good EPK.

I have to say that radio is a harder medium to crack as the programming schedule is decided by the editorial team and will mostly consist of established bands already in the top 40. I think it would be a waste of time and resources sending promo material to loads of radio stations you will not have a chance of getting onto, or gaining any airplay.

## WHO TO SEND YOUR PUBLICITY TO

Each major town will have a university press and radio department. Each uni will also have its own radio station along with the uni magazine. As they want to be seen as the anti-establishment and the bastions of cool, you do stand a very good chance of having your single played and your band covered in print. Also, your local town will have its own daily newspaper or two. This is the basis of starting your press company as you will have the contact information to get your music to those who can deliver it to the public. That's what the big media company guns do. They have a national database of contacts covering all the relevant media people they need to talk to. Don't go thinking the big guys succeed every time in getting all their bands national or local coverage. They don't. So don't think because you are just starting out you don't stand a chance, you do, every bit as much as anyone else. And you won't be paying over £1,000 per month for the privilege either.

## Building your database

So, when you are about to release your album or plan a tour, first think of the towns you will be playing and when the dates are confirmed make a list of those towns. If you can, get a good database program, one like Microsoft Access is good but to be honest it always frustrated me. In reality it didn't have the coolness that I had in my mind. Guess I wanted a James Bond-style database program. So I opted to use Outlook for my entire database and contact info. Using Outlook means you can cross reference contact info with email and journal programs. It means in the space of a tour campaign you can keep records of who you spoke to, what the outcome was, what emails you sent and received, along with keeping you very organised indeed. That's my preference and it works for me. I have a database of contacts that span over 3,000 people worldwide and it makes my life easier when it comes to remembering what's been arranged and is a great way to look back and see how you can improve on your data management skills.

I would advocate keeping a diary to remind you of what you are doing. It will get very crazy very quickly and it's easy to forget a few things. Like anything else, practice will make you an expert in double quick time.

## Approaching the press

You now have your town and city information. When you are approaching the press guys, but you are not really sure of the best way, use this template until you find your own style.

Firstly each newspaper will have a journalist who takes care of the music news. This will either be a dedicated member of staff or one or two who will do it when it's a bad news day. Either way it will be a regular name and it's up to you to find who out who that person is. Go online and access the newspaper and see if music articles are published, and make a note of that person.

Have your tour dates ready along with other relevant info so you know what you are about to say. Call the newspaper. You will get through to reception.

*Good afternoon, The Rock and Roll Times.*

If you know the journo's name this is what you say:

*Hi can I speak to Tony Montana?*

*Putting you through.*

You will feel slightly nervous if you haven't done this much but after a few times you will be fine with it. Stick to the points and don't oversell it. They will sniff an amateur out instantly.

Ring ring.

*Music News.*

*Hi is that Tony Montana?*

*Yes it is.*

*My name is Clint Eastwood. I'm the press agent for The Bananas, a local band, do you have a minute or an email I can take to send you some information?*

At this point the journo will either prefer you to send an email or you might be lucky and get a chat, in which case still get an email. The point is to not unload all the information in one go, as they will be dealing with 30 calls a day. Best to make an easy impression first go and build from there. It seems a little silly writing that scenario but that's exactly what you will experience when you do it. If you don't know the name of the journalist when you get through to the reception then politely ask them who deals with the music news. Make a note and then ask them, if they haven't already asked, to be put through to that person. Most local journalists are actually very happy to help out bands and you won't find it too difficult to make contact. As with everything else, it's the space that is a premium and you will be in contest with other bands. So make sure you plan far enough ahead to give yourself an edge. Most music pages will be written and filed a week or two before publication. You won't get many last minute dot coms in the print world at a local band level.

*Approaching uni press and radio*

It's the same when approaching uni press and radio. Find out who you need to talk to and go talk to them. It sounds ridiculously easy saying all this, but there is no magic kingdom to fight through, no promised land, just organisation, a polite manner and a phone number or email. Once you have established contact you can then send through what you need. That will be a CD, press pack containing the band bio, web address and forthcoming gigs. It really is that easy.

# BREAKING INTO MUSIC JOURNALISM

If you want to become a music journalist then I advise you to start off with a course. Most local colleges will run a City and Guilds qualification in journalism. It's a great foundation to greater things and will give you the fundamentals in media techniques. After I completed the course I was on I bypassed further education and got straight into a music column. I had realised that the local newspaper in my town at the point, Colchester, didn't really have a hard and fast music column. So I spent a month reading the *Evening Gazette* every day to study which day there was a music page and who wrote it. After my investigation was complete it was obvious there wasn't a full-time staffer or anyone dedicated to writing the music page and those who did were not really that cutting edge.

So I wrote a letter to the editor at that time explaining how it would be a very good addition for the paper to have a regular weekly music column for the kids. I pointed out all the strengths of a music column supporting the local music scene and how the paper for whatever reason wasn't supporting that. And considering Colchester gave birth to Blur, it was the newspaper's responsibility to support a vibrant and healthy scene with a vibrant and healthy music column. Off went the letter and two days later I had a call from the editor telling me to go ahead and create the new music column. One week after that I had reviews from local bands in that column, along with an interview with Metallica and a review of what was at that point their latest album before it hit the shops.

## Setting up a career

The column was a full page and set me up in my career and it's really the best way to get started. This was before the internet really kicked in with ezines, fanzines and numerous online magazines. It got me into contact with media companies, record labels and bands from all over the world. All of a sudden I had Iron Maiden and Ozzy Osbourne calling my house from wherever they were in the world doing phone interviews for the following week's edition. I went out every night to the local music venue and got to know everyone. I'd be up till 2am watching bands then getting home to write the copy for the column. I'd spend the day talking to record labels about new bands and creating interviews for new press campaigns. I saw MUSE when they first started out playing to ten people and having their press guy asking me if I'd go easy on them because they were so nervous. If only the press guy knew how nervous I was! I learned also that media companies could become complacent in their attitudes. Some were on the ball and some weren't. I'd get all the latest and new releases to review and get tickets to gigs. I became quite popular with people after that...

It's also where I leaned how the industry works. I had so many bands come through with great albums playing to an empty hall, only for them to be dropped by their label six months after due to the public not taking hold. Looking back it was a great education as I was in the trenches with these bands. I'd interview them outside in their cars, freezing on a cold winter's night, and getting to know how they became signed and what plans were set for them. This is the stage where you are still innocent and it's a great place to be. You only love the music and bands. You watch bands play live, you hear their new album and you write about it. If this is what you love, stay there. Once you get further into the industry your innocence is taken away from you and it never quite feels the same.

If I hadn't taken that step or initiative to believe in what I could do, then I would not have got that column. I probably had no more experience than you have now, but I did have belief and faith. And that was all I needed. Oh, and passion, I had tons of that!

# Making Your Video

Making videos used to be out of reach for most bands. But once again our friend the digital technology revolution has enabled all of us to make videos, whatever quality, for next to nothing. I will not buy any excuse from any band who complains about not having the resources to do at least some kind of video work. Most families in the UK will either have a home digicam or access to one. Mobile phones have capabilities to record video footage and whilst the quality isn't up to broadcast standards you can record something. Once again it's down to the individual band's savvy.

## THE EQUIPMENT

Digital camcorders cost from £200 pounds upwards and all you have to do is shoot and film everything a band does from rehearsals to gigs to interviews to life on the road. Out of all this footage you will be able to put together a video for your first single. Just like the music software it will only take time to get to grips. Video editing software is quite inexpensive so again there is no excuse. You can even download fully functioning trial software for 30 days so there is your first step to guerrilla video shooting. The big Hollywood style shots that have cost previous bands thousands of pounds have done nothing other than eat into their royalties and bankrupted record labels. The days of the million dollar video budgets are over. It boils down to your own creativity as to how anything you do turns out.

## KEEPING COSTS DOWN

Once again, if you are at university go and say hi to the movie school kids. Most college courses running film and video studies will need projects so it's worth enquiring if you can get them to do a video for the band. Pass out free tickets to your next gig in return. The point is that there will be some way for you to deliver on videos for the band. Great video editing software includes Final Cut Pro for the Mac **www.apple.com** and Premier Pro for the PC **www.adobe.com**. Pinnacle and Sony also have software for more restricted budgets.

This chapter was never going to be long or technical, but to just give you some ideas of what you can do without spending huge fortunes. I've known bands to make videos for £20. There is one band on the internet that has a video of just a head-banging beaver shot entirely in the band's front room. It's that simple. I have to say I've deliberately not mentioned video production companies. You are looking at anything upwards to £2,000 for a location shoot and storyboard. This is fine when you are signed and have money backing you. But if you have a small budget you are always better off investing in your own equipment and producing your own mini videos. If you don't have the time then recruit a fan to film you everywhere. Once you have it in the can then your next stop is your website and YouTube.

# Setting Up a Record Label

Commandment Nine
**Setting up your very own Record label...**

Creating a record label is an easy thing to do. It's the money-making that's the hard part. You need to eat, live and reinvest to continue what could be a dream come true to anyone who dares to go down this road. Bands are finding themselves in a position where they can sell over 100,000 albums and have still not recouped their investment due to the amount of promotional costs they have sustained from a record label blanket bombing the public with a new band/album release. I don't want to get into music industry politics because ultimately it's very boring and whilst there is major change coming to the old music business model it is still a few years away.

## CHANGES IN THE MUSIC INDUSTRY

You are, however, in the midst of that change and no matter what you read or hear from the men in suits it will be you, the band, the music fan that will determine that change. You have led the internet revolution and you will lead it again. It won't be the so-called tastemakers, or the think tank experts, or media savvy luvvies, it will be the kids on the street, the kids with dreams, in their bedrooms, who will hit upon the next idea that will bring change to all our lives.

Apple's iTunes is the biggest single digital distributor in existence. It was a damning disgrace on the part of the music industry to not see this coming; that only confirms where the future is heading. Record labels will adapt, they will change and they will still be here in the future. It's the *how* they will adapt that remains to be seen. The new music industry business model will be based on record labels signing bands not only to record deals but to merchandise, management and touring. Some labels will tie in strategic relationships with media companies such as games makers, TV and movie sync companies, making the new business model very attractive to new bands. You can expect to see smaller labels do this before the big guns finally wake and place their new music in a particular brand of coffee store. This business model is already in place with labels like **www.nettwerk.com** who are based in Canada.

## Finding a new way

Most bands still harbour that dream where a big A&R guy will descend from the heavens with a great record deal and make them famous. Those bands think that only signing a deal will bring validation to their lives and careers. I'm not interested in arguing the toss regarding what bands think is best for them. People have a habit of learning the hard way and being signed doesn't guarantee success. Record labels take the financial risk when they sign you and take all of your rights along with it. Until the second you recoup the money invested you will not see a penny or be able to buy your mamma that house she's now got her eye on. Most bands will never recoup and end up with their careers owing money, that won't be returnable unless you have success later, and not even owning the music they wrote.

I can already see where this is leading me so I will pull back from the brink before I go crazy. It will become very evident very quickly to a band whether a record label is interested or not. And if they are not then setting up your own label is what you should do. If you have any brains, this is what you should do anyway. And if you fancy yourself as a record company mogul then please step into my office.

This guide will show bands as well as potential record execs how to put the basic infrastructure of a label together. If you're a band and you've funded everything so far yourselves then the beauty of this is that you will own 100 per cent of your empire. If you're an individual and have set up a label and have signed an artist then you will own the rights, and pay the artists according to the royalty rate and type of deal you have put together. This is where I find myself in two minds. Do I write this from a band perspective and how they should set themselves up, or do I write from an entrepreneur perspective and fly the corporate flag, because ultimately that's what a label will become whether you like or not. Or you will go bust!

## I'm still thinking…

God damn there is no revolution without the revolutionaries. I'm going to write this from the bands' perspective. The entrepreneurs out there will be able to take the basics here and apply them to a business model. You should understand that the record label business model in the future will be a cross collateralised platform where labels put up the money to break/fund and develop bands that will include recording, promotion, managing, merch and other media platforms for a straight 20 per cent cut across the board. Now, the men in suits reading this right now are probably choking on their cornflakes or are thinking I've put a bit too much crack on mine, but despite the financial per cent I've mentioned, this type of deal is the future of the industry.

If you are setting up a label outside of being in a band then you will need to understand this. From the band's perspective the reason you need to consider setting up your own label is that it makes you more professional. You are running a business which hopefully you can make a living from, and you can grow and invest to develop the business further. Setting up a company will be the best way to protect yourselves legally and financially. It also means that whilst you pay for everything you will own everything and recoup. You will never do that when you sign to a major label. Not ever.

## HOW TO DO IT

There are chapters in this book that deal in depth with some of the specific areas linked to setting up a label and will not need to be repeated. When it comes to legal and accountancy advice, as always go and seek the word of the professionals, you will have to anyway, and it will save you time, money and heartache in the long run. Should you create a record label and having proven its worth by selling a good number of CDs, merch, selling out gigs, etc (from the band's perspective), you won't really need to sell hundreds of thousands of product to make a living and you may attract financial investment to take things to the next level. It's very attractive to a bigger company to see a start-up generate income and prove its worth by establishing a fan base that is loyal and consistently comes back to buy more stuff.

When I mention merch I'm really going back to band's thinking about developing clothing lines. Don't go thinking you have to be a major clothing company to get clothes made. Not everyone wants a name brand on their clothes and those that do, especially when they are younger, want their favourite band's name on their caps, rucksacks and jeans…

## Choose the name

The first step is to choose a record company name. That is solely down to you my friends, make it a good one, something that reaches out and makes a statement, something cool and something that tells the world about who you are. I've seen companies choose names which at the time they thought were funny only to have to change them a year or more later. Dumb move, as this will cost the company in many ways, not just financial, but in rebranding which never seems to work out. Leave the funny names to the movies as real life will only be far too politically correct for them to work for you. Make sure that whatever name you have chosen isn't already out there and double check that the web domain is available.

## Website

You then need to go and register the website. You will have already made sure the web domain is available because if it isn't then what's the frickin point? A lot of the media presence you have will derive from the website along with your shop. There are many hosting companies, do your own research, who will offer deals that include multiple domain registrations, so you can register the .coms and .co.uk along with whatever else you think is relevant.

## Register the company

Head over to www.uk-plc.net/companyformation/ to form a company. Read all the information thoroughly before choosing which one to opt for. A limited company will be the best option but it's not up to me to tell you which to go for. It will depend on your requirements and how deep you want to go. Starting costs are around £25. Then go to www.companieshouse.gov.uk to register the company and to list the director and company secretary. There is tons of info for you to digest and as potential business people you will need to learn and understand. Don't be daunted by this as it should be viewed as an exciting time. You're taking the power. The initial costs are £20 and will take around five days to get set up. You have taken the first steps to turning that dream into reality.

## YOUR OFFICE SET-UP

Most costs in running any business go on running an office and whilst initially this will be out of reach to most of you it's not an impossibility when it comes to the internet. Remember you are a start up, beginning a new adventure, and no one ever said you had to waltz into plush offices in the best part of town to give you any kind of credibility. I knew a label once that had been given a million pounds to set themselves up. They knew nothing about the music industry and thought money was the answer to creating success. They rented offices in Hyde Park at a cost of thousands before they even set up the infrastructure. Big mistake number 1. They then signed a pop idol reject band. Big mistake number 2. They then had staff that wasted loads of money on expenses. I watched them do this, as they ran around trying to be the new kings on the block. Big mistake number 3. It wasn't long before the accounts people stepped in and put an end to this madness, but it was too late. A total mismanagement from beginning to end and these people were supposed to be businessmen.

So, don't be intimidated by anything or anyone. You're not expected to be fantastic straight out of the box. Instead, you are building something from the ground up. Using the internet this is how you can create and run an office with the resources you will already have.

### The internet

You simply run everything from your computer. Everyone now has the internet at home. If you don't then there isn't a phone company in existence that doesn't offer a great deal with fantastic download speeds for moving files and downloading all the music and movies you like. Many of you will have deals in place already and if you are coming up to the end of a contract then you will get a new company offering you the earth just to get your custom. So, you have the internet and that's where you start.

### Skype

You head over to www.skype.com and download the program. Those who don't know what Skype is are in for a treat. Skype is a software program that was designed for people to call each other using the software over the internet for free. The website will explain everything you need to know and it's a program more and more businesses are starting to use as it saves them huge costs. There are costs to call landlines and mobile phones, but these are minimal and you can call anywhere on the planet for the same price. There are various packages according to your needs and it's free to download and get started. You will need a VoIP (voice over internet protocol) phone, but you can buy one of these quite cheaply for around £20. The beauty in this program is that you can buy a landline telephone number even with the area code you want, London, Manchester, Glasgow, etc, for people to call you. This would be your office number and when you are busy or not online there is a voicemail service.

With the Skype Pro package you can get set up to be called wherever you are in the world along with calls being forwarded to your mobile. Anyone using Skype can call you for free and anyone using a regular phone will pay regular tariffs. As it's a digital service the reception is as good as it gets. You can conference call up to 50 people and use the instant messaging service to communicate with anyone in your address book. This already gives you a professional edge and it's a must-have addition to your office.

## Mobile phone

I would endorse the Blackberry range for being away from the computer and having instant access to your emails. It's another tool for you to consider and will not cost you any more than the tariff you are paying already. You can start with a Blackberry tariff from www.vodaphone.co.uk that will be around £25 per month. If you want a combination of phone, text and Blackberry then a good deal is £50 per month and is worth the outlay. Deals differ all the time so again, you will have to do some up-to-date research. The beauty of the Blackberry is that it frees you from the computer and if you are out on the road awaiting important emails then you can do so without the hassle of finding an internet café. It adds to your professionalism as you build and grow your business. It's really all about time management as you can expect to get very busy very quickly. And for all those people who deem technology as millstones, well there is always the off button!

## Address and post

You need to think about security. You don't really want fans/potential head-cases turning up on your doorstep at 3am singing your songs or demanding to see you. And your mamma isn't going to like that. There's nothing more guaranteed to give your granny/dog/budgie a heart attack than some loony banging on your door asking for a record deal. So, it's worth getting a PO box number to use for mail. www.royalmail.com has all the details you need to get set up. The cost is around £60 for a year and is worth the investment. So you now have an address and a phone number to start trading. You are essentially set up in business now.

## MAKING THE CD READY FOR MARKET

## PPL

www.ppluk.com

Phonographic Performance Limited is a music industry organisation that collects and distributes airplay and public performance royalties in the UK. Anywhere a song is played, whether TV, radio, internet radio, clubs, pubs or bars, PPL will collect a royalty and distribute it to its members consisting of record companies and performers. So if you are a record label in the making you will need to apply for membership. Once your application has been processed and you have songs played in the public arena you will be entitled to royalties. You will have access to CatCo, which is the music industry sound recording database that will allow you to submit all new release data electronically. Membership is free and for a more detailed breakdown for your education go visit, learn, and then join the PPL.

You will then be given an IRSC identifier, the international standard numbering code that is encoded into your tracks/recordings which identifies the track as belonging to you, the owner, and track usage of the music. An IRSC code is generally embedded when it comes to burning your master CD before you get it replicated. Think of the IRSC as the key to collecting royalties for recordings in the digital information age. The IRSC is a tool for the purpose of rights administration and electronic distribution of music.

## Pressing and merch

Once you have your CDs pressed and merchandise set up you are ready to go and can now start to sell. Getting it to the public requires distribution and as you, again, have already read the chapter on distribution you have options to decide which way is best for you.

## Business plan

It's around this point you may start to consider putting together a business plan to seek further investment. First make sure you have something to sell and a story to help sell it. Up till now everything will have been an expense, so make sure you keep receipts for everything. You will offset this against tax. There are software programs that help you develop business plans and are a good way to help you if you haven't got the expertise to write a professional plan. www.businessplanpro.com has a UK edition along with templates to help you understand the procedure of writing a professional plan to submit to a potential investor.

Depending on how far along you are with the development of your label will determine how and when you want to submit a plan. It's worth seeking the services of a lawyer and an accountant. There is a chapter on each and how they can help you, so if you haven't read them then you have that coming.

## Accounts

You can help yourself further by getting hold of an accountancy program to keep tabs on your sales. www.sage.com or www. quickbooks.com are two professional accountancy programs that will get your accounts into shape before you have to start paying for the services of a professional accountant. You should get into the frame of mind if you are selling on a regular basis to keep accounts in shape at least weekly. It will save you heartache in the long run. And, at some point, the taxman will come knocking. They will not accept ignorance as an excuse and you are serious about making a living from music, right? Then you need to be professional. And that means looking after your business. It will determine what kind of life you want.

The more seriously you take it the better the chances of succeeding. An accountant will advise you on the breaks you are entitled to and will end up saving you money. Anyone who is self-employed needs an accountant. Businesses need accountants and you will need an accountant. Hey, I thought this was the fun part? It is, but you still need to be professional.

## SELLING YOUR WARES

### Distribution

Read the distribution chapter on the options you have available. It will mostly be on the digital platform to begin with as well as selling CDs and merch at gigs. I would approach a distributor with a detailed PR plan along with previous sales to see what kind of response you get. But to start with I would focus on selling through your website and gigs. www.paypal.co.uk is the financial business transaction site to use to sell your products. To set an account up is free and with different types of accounts available you can choose what suits you best. If you have used eBay, and most of us have, then you will know the drill. If you want some one else to take care of the business side then I suggest www.ukbands.net who have set up a webpage for bands to sell merch and CDs along with whatever else you can create. Be it DVD or ring tones you will have a set page named ukbands.net/yourbandname which you can link to your website for fans to access. You have plenty of options now so what are you waiting for? Oh, you want to make some coffee?

## MCPS-PRS and PPL

Once activity surrounds the label and band you will need to join a royalty collection society like MCPS-PRS and the PPL. All the info concerning the benefits of these societies have been men-tioned in depth elsewhere. Hopefully you have read those chapters or you are about to. As a professional organisation you will need to join these organisations, PRS as a performer and MCPS along with PPL as a label. Easy, isn't it?

## VPL

www.vpluk.com

At some point you will be making videos, either for the band, or for the label itself. Either way you will need to join the VPL. VPL stands for Video Performance Limited and is a collecting society set up by the recording industry to grant licences to users of music videos, like broadcaster-music programs, program makers and any platform that broadcasts music videos. The membership is free to anyone who owns the rights to a music video, whether a company or individual, with incomes fees collected from the end user of those videos. So, if you get a video broadcast and you are a member then you should be entitled to a royalty. For more detailed info head over to the website and check everything out. There is even a number to call to chat to someone in the membership department.

## Press and publicity

By now you will know how to set up your own press team. The band itself will have generated a buzz or at least be on their way to generating it. You will be thinking about the specific music magazines to target, along with webzines and web internet radio stations. Any time the band are gigging you will set up a press campaign that will identify and target the university media in that town, along with the local newspaper music column. The band should have a good list of fans to email. Invite journalists down to review the gig and interview the band, and make sure if you can to film any footage to go towards future videos. Set a stall up to sell CDs and merch. Don't roar up on the day of the gig expecting people to turn up if you haven't given enough time to get people organised. They won't show. So, once the gigs are booked, start the planning of any press in advance. A couple of weeks is

> **Proper planning and preparation prevents piss poor performance.**

around the time frame to organise this. There is a good army moto that I like to use. It's called the seven P's. Proper planning and preparation prevents piss poor performance. And it tends to work.

## STARTING TO SELL

So that's about it. You now have the foundation to set yourself up as a record label. The rest of course is you having to really understand the aspects of running a record label and that, my friends, is through experience and actually doing it. Don't underestimate how far your passion can take you but make sure you run it professionally too. Half the battle sometimes can be based on the belief that setting a label up needs a ton of money and complete expertise. But let's not point out the obvious, we are intelligent people, we are creative too.

You are at the seedling stage now. Don't expect too much too soon. You will need an accountant and a solicitor to oversee the business, financial and legal side but the rest is down to your own creativity. Once you start signing bands, you will be the A&R guy, you will be the one spending the money, and you will be responsible for steering the ship. The sense of empowerment this will give you may well be new in your life. Unless you get a massive injection of finance you will be starting small. Then once you start to sell you will see your label grow to a point where you can add more bands to the roster. Every label you have ever heard about started where you are today.

First, you have the dream. Second, you have the means to set it up. And third, you have access to the artists. Every year a new crop of bands are formed. Every year you have a chance to be the first to sign what could be the making of your new record company. The point is that you do have a fighting chance. You are in a remarkable time to set up a label due to digital technology. The media industry has exploded these past few years and it is one industry that will continue to expand. People will always want to be entertained. Dramatic developments in technology and software will make the best professional platforms open to everyone. That means we all have a chance at building a dream into a reality for very little cost.

The motivation, belief and determination to succeed can only come from within. So don't let yourself be intimidated by anything or anyone. Never let another person tell you it can't be done. I'm telling you it can. And I look forward to seeing it happen, people. Drop me a line sometime and let me know how you are getting on. And remember, Who Dares Wins!

# How to Set Up a Festival

Commandment Ten

# END OF THE ROAD FESTIVAL

www.endoftheroadfestival.com

www.myspace.com/endoftheroadfestival

What's wonderful about life is that sometimes it can surprise you. In the context of this book I had a blueprint to cover a variety of subjects. Not all of those subjects made it, some were cut, and some were added. This chapter was the one real surprise I never would have dreamed of including because setting up a new festival seems so outrageous. But it can be done, even if you do need a huge set of kahunas to pull it off. The End of the Road Festival is held in the Dorset/Wiltshire borders and is now two years old. Operating without a corporate flag, the festival is a new type of breed where you won't see huge advertising billboards, or any kind of corporate sponsorship. I think the festival retains a lovely kind of innocence and with that in mind I wanted to convey the story of how the event came to be.

So I'm happy to hand over to Sofia Hagberg to tell you in her own words how they came up with the idea and how they executed the plan. I hope it serves as an inspiration to all of you who harbour any kind of dream to be involved in the music industry. I've orchestrated the plan from idea and conception to execution.

## The idea

It all started at the Green Man festival in August 2005. Myself (Sofia) and two friends, Simon and Jason, travelled down from London to Wales to the Green Man festival, which we had only really heard of on the grapevine until Bonnie Prince Billy was announced as one of the headliners – that's when we decided to go.

The Green Man festival in 2005 probably had about 3,000 people there, and it was so intimate and beautiful. The organisation was very simple with a small presence of stewards/security – which gave it a lovely community feel. You would walk around and bump into the same people numerous times every day, which meant that you made ten times more friends than you would at bigger festivals such as Glastonbury.

Simon saw all this and started to think if it might be possible to do a festival himself. This was a bit of a crazy idea that he had been playing around with before, but never really thought it realistic until now. He sat in the field and did some calculations on his mobile and then it took him another month after the festival to share his ideas with the rest of us. Simon had run the idea past a few people who were involved in the music industry, and got some positive response and he had also contacted a few agents with regards to bands – so now it was time to get the ball rolling. He had been racking his brain to come up with the perfect partner in crime, and no one came to mind as the obvious one – until one day he picked up the phone and ran the idea past me. My response was so enthusiastic Simon made up his mind there and then that this was it! This was the chance to live the dream and turn an amazing and creative idea into reality.

## The licence

Simon had already done some of the groundwork by contacting contractors to get quotes on things like toilets, stages, security, etc... and then the hard work of getting the licence started.

Getting the licence is quite a serious and fairly complicated business, so we needed someone on board that the Licensing Authority would take seriously and this is how Philip (Simon's book keeper) joined the team.

And to give you the bigger picture of this team, Simon is a painter and decorator, I was a Secretary/PA and Philip runs various businesses and is a book keeper. None of us had ever done anything within music before (apart from Simon's DJing).

Between September 2005 and February 2006, we spent every weekend and most nights working away on the licence, creating site plans, finding suitable contractors and the most important thing – booking bands.

## Finding advice

One of the first things we did was to identify other festivals which we might be able to go to for advice and help, as we had planned on paying them on a consultancy basis. A lot of them unfortunately didn't have the time, or didn't reply at all – but we had very helpful responses from Ashton Court Festival, the Secret Garden Party, Bestival, Wychwood, Blissfields, Glastonbury and Emmaboda (Sweden).

Just before Christmas we managed to take on a Site Manager in Steve Hunt (who organises Ashton Court Festival) and a Health and Safety (H&S) Officer in Anna Dolan (who has worked on Wychwood amongst other festivals). We didn't actually end up using any of the contacts as a consultant, they were all so very kind to offer advice over the email whenever we had questions to ask. Amazing!

It took us from September 2005 until the end of March and one formal hearing with the Licensing Authority to finally get the licence. But as this was our first time, there were certain aspects that we had missed out and we had to apply for variations (which is lengthy and costly), so it is important to seek advice and get the application right from the start.

## THE CONCEPT

We have always joked around saying that wouldn't it be nice to put on our own 'perfect' festival with our favourite line-up, and to include all the things that are important to us at festivals, such as:

- you won't get all the over-hyped bands headlining
- most bands play longer sets
- you can eat a range of quality food
- you can drink a range of quality beers, ales and cider
- the security guards are decent people, who show respect to everyone
- the crowd will be there for the music.

So, the idea with the End of the Road Festival was to organise an intimate festival with our favourite artists, and to offer the bands an opportunity to play longer sets, compared to most other festivals. The festival would have a friendly and relaxed feel. The music we were putting on would attract a music-loving, open minded and chilled-out crowd. We found the Larmer Tree Gardens (North Dorset, UK) would be the perfect venue to create this kind of atmosphere

## Creative freedom

We wanted the End of the Road festival to take a lot of interest in all the 'little things' that make a great festival, such as good food (organic/local), good beer, caring and well-mannered staff, hygiene, etc.

So we decided to avoid sponsorships in order to keep our creative freedom, and to avoid littering the beautiful venue with commercial banners. (Therefore, we are so grateful to all bands who come for the fun of it and who play for a smaller fee than they are used to.)

The aim was to involve the bands as much as possible, giving room for bands to DJ, hold workshops and show films. We also planned to set up a marquee to show various films and workshops of our own choice throughout the weekend.

Also, hailing from Sweden I wanted a Scandinavian feel to the festival, giving bands from Sweden, Norway, Denmark, Finland and Iceland a chance to play too.

## INFORMATION

The End of the Road festival now caters for about 5,000 people, and the very first one took place between the 15–17th September 2006 and this is the initial information that we put up on our website for that year. The gardens open in the afternoon on the Friday, with the first bands starting to play around 6pm. There are two full festival days on Saturday and Sunday, with bands starting around 12pm and finishing at midnight.

The Larmer Tree Gardens is about 2.5-3 hours drive from London, on the border between North Dorset and Wiltshire, close to Stonehenge. It's a beautiful venue with peacocks and huge parrots roaming/flying around freely both inside the gardens and in the field. A big top with a capacity of 2,500 will put on DJ sets at night, after the live music has finished. A small acoustic tent/stage is also available where anyone is welcome to play, including festival goers – like an ongoing jam session. This stage will also be open to all kinds of artists, whether it's reading poetry, doing stand-up comedy or yodelling. There is a merchandise stall available, where all bands are welcome to sell their merchandise, and we don't charge them for this as we want to support the artists as much as possible.

## The music

Music-wise it's very hard to tell you what type of music we will have because it's so varied and we have long ago lost faith in the word 'indie'. So instead of trying to describe it all, we will simply list some of the musicians/bands on our ideal Wish List. We had planned to have a few biggish headliners, but we also want to encourage new music! So a lot of the bands may be ones that most people have never heard of, but who will hopefully be off to a good start at the End of the Road Festival.

Confirming the bands was going to be a gradual process, as unfortunately we don't have the buying power of the big festivals to announce all bands overnight.

This was our first 'announcement' of confirmed bands on the website, on 27.03.2006.

My Latest Novel, The Boy Least Likely To, Ralfe Band, Absentee, The Bright Space, Chris T-T and Crosbi. A lot more to come.

*Original wishlist (in no particular order)*

| | |
|---|---|
| Sigur Rós | The Concretes |
| Badly Drawn Boy | Architecture in Helsinki |
| Beck | King Creosote |
| Nick Cave | Four Tet |

PJ Harvey

Super Furry Animals

Arcade Fire

Devendra Banhart

Anthony and the Johnson's

Flaming Lips

My Latest Novel

Mercury Rev

Wilco

Yo La Tengo

Animal Collective

My Morning Jacket

M Ward

Black Mountain

Richard Hawley

Wolf Parade

Superthriller

Clap Your Hands, Say Yeah

Black Keys

Martha Wainwright

Modest Mouse

Shins

Sufjan Stevens

Tom Vek

Brendan Benson

The National

Sophie Zelmani

Mogwai

Euros Childs

The Czars

Guillemots

Jeffrey Lewis

Soundtrack of Our Lives

Adam Green

Smog

British Sea Power

Richard Buckner

King Biscuit Time

Charlie Parr

Pip Dylan

Mike Fellows

Holly Golightly

Kings of Convenience

Crosbi

Dan Sartain

Square Pusher

My Brightest Diamond

CocoRosie

Sons and Daughters

Ladytron

Mountain Goats

Imogen Heap

Bob Hund/Bergman Rock

Wannadies

Jamie Lidell

The Boy Least Likely To

Ladyfuzz

Buff Medways

Magnolia Electric Company

Sleater Kinney

Holy F*ck

Neko Case

Belle & Sebastian

Kelley Stoltz

Bob Log III

Tunng

Anna Ternheim

Love Is All

Sunny Day Sets Fire

Ramblin' Jack Elliott

Scout Niblett

Bell Orchestre

Paris Motel

Jens Lekman

Matson Jones

Archie Bronson Outfit

Rocky Votolato

Regina Spektor

Jeremy Warmsley

Built To Spill

Hot Chip

## Links

- **Venue**: Larmer Tree Gardens
  www.larmertreegardens.co.uk

- **Festival**:
  www.endoftheroadfestival.com

- **MySpace**:
  www.myspace.com/endoftheroadfestival

- **Kubb**:
  www.vikingkubb.co.uk

## FINDING A VENUE

Planning where to hold a festival includes various aspects – you want it to be easy for people to get to, you want the site to be fairly flat so that it is safe for structures such as stages, you want it to be easily accessed by forklift trucks, etc, you want it to be beautiful, you want it to be the right size and so on…

But we took none of the above into consideration when starting to look for a venue. Simon simply did a search on Google, putting in 'festival site for hire'… all we really knew was that the ideal location for the festival would be somewhere between London and

Brighton. The Google search literally came up with only a few options and the first one Simon looked at was the Larmer Tree Gardens. He drove down there a couple of days later, and fell in love with the site and that was it!

Simon and I then had to book an appointment with the trust who owns the land/gardens, and present to them our plan and our vision, and show them that we are reliable people who know what we're doing. At the time, we obviously didn't know what we were doing – but we learnt as we went along and the lovely people at the Larmer Tree Gardens/Saville's had faith in us and have been a great support since.

The site hire fee was also something that we needed to negotiate, and they gave us a base figure and then an additional fee based on ticket sales, which is fair. It is always good to check other festival sites, to find out how much they pay in rent, so that you don't end up paying far too much.

## Setting a date

When booking a venue allow enough time for build-up and take-down (this is crucial). Setting the date for an event should include looking at factors such as:

- What else is going on in the area at the same time.

- What else is going on in general at the same time, other similar events, for example the Football World Cup!

- Weather forecasts for this time of year.

- If the date allows you enough time to plan and execute the event successfully.

Again, we didn't have much choice as the only two free weekends that the Larmer Tree Gardens had to offer us were either early May 2006 or mid-September 2006. We knew that there was no chance for us to have anything ready for a festival in May – so it had to be September. We did check the weather reports for this weekend, going back five years, and it was surprisingly sunny and warm – so we decided to go ahead.

Anyone in general starting out a new project/event in a field that they have no experience in would be mad to think that they can do it in just one year! But we had a lot of passion and strong beliefs that we could do it – and so we did! In hindsight, we would definitely advise anyone planning to organise a festival to start at least two years in advance.

## Build-up and take-down times

As the Larmer Tree Gardens itself is used as a wedding venue all year round, the weekends are when they have their best income and this would affect our access to the site before and after the festival. We had to negotiate build-up and take-down times, and we have learnt from last year that we need more than just five or six days before the festival for build-up. For an event of our scale (small, compared to some festivals) we are now looking to access the site at least eight to ten days before the festival is due to start. The site and all the structures etc will need to be checked and given the go-ahead by the licensing authority – usually the day before it opens to the public, and then one last check on the day to allow for any changes based on the check from the day before.

Take-down is much quicker than the build-up and for our size of event, it was all cleared two to four days after. Don't forget your litter-pickers, as you want to leave the site as beautiful as it was before you hired it!

## Production manager

You need to find a production manager (although, we didn't), or at least your H&S officer. There are lots of event management companies around, but it's important to find someone with the relevant experience in the field you're in. We were recommended Chris Tarren by the Wychwood festival and that was good enough for us. Philip met up with Chris on site and straight away, he knew that Chris was our man! He literally saved the festival, as our plans for the site were far too big – he even managed to take off one whole stage, which saved us a fortune. It is really important not to try to do *everything* in the first year!

A production manager should have great communication skills, experience from similar events and also needs to have a load of certificates, etc. It is also important that you like the person and that you get along, as during the festival itself you will be living in each other's pockets and will have to work together through ups and downs.

This is the company that Chris Tarren works for, to give you an idea of the credentials/background, etc: http://www.eandms.com/

With regards to H&S – it is also very important that the person has had previous experience of the type of event that you're planning to hold, and you also need to check their certificates, etc. Again, Anna came recommended by Graeme at Wychwood, which was great.

## Contacts

Source contacts with experience to ask for help approaching the music industry. We did not to do this to any set formula, it was mainly just based on talking to people at gigs and gradually building a network of friends/contacts in the industry. It's a lot smaller world than one thinks!

The best thing we did was to go to South By South West in Austin, Texas. Again, it was Simon, Jason and myself… the good old gig and festival going team! We were armed with info packs about the festival and we would talk to everyone we met about the festival and this is where most of our industry contacts came from. SXSW is also very good from a band point of view, as almost all the up-and-coming artists play there and it's very easy to chat to the bands/artists directly. The personal contact and the passion with which we describe the festival really seems to make a difference to the bands.

We were very lucky to have real friends who happen to be in the industry from before we started this crazy idea and they have been immensely helpful. Apart from meeting people face to face, there are always books that can be very helpful for contacts of any kind, whether you want to find an agent, a promoter, a venue, management, etc – two publications that we find really useful are the *White Book* and *Music Week's Directory*.

## Your licence

The earlier you start to apply for a licence the better. You need to find out within which county your venue is located geographically, and then contact the Licensing Authority within that county. Usually the details are very easy to find on the county's homepage or you can phone the regional tourist board to find out.

Our festival site is a bit funny, as the garden itself is in Wiltshire and the field is in Dorset… but on the recommendation from the venue we contacted Dorset and they have been very helpful from day one.

## Book bands

I left my job as a PA to focus 100 per cent on the festival in February 2006, and my main task was to book all the bands. Never having done anything like this, we didn't know that all bands have agents – so it all started with a hectic schedule of running round to shows and gigs with handwritten cards for the bands that we wanted at the festival, including some information on our vision of the festival.

Gradually we got to know a lot of the agents, mainly via email, as they are very busy people who (most of them, not all) prefer to be in contact over email rather than over the telephone or in person.

When it comes to booking bands it isn't always a case of the agent having a hard and fast set fee. Bands always need to play and get exposure and sometimes it's better for them to play a gig to get exposure to a new audience than for an agent to haggle. Agents will always try to get the best fees for their bands which means you will find yourself in a position of having to make the first offer before real negotiations can begin. If you have no experience in booking bands you will have to guess how much a band is worth. From the agent's point of view this will indicate how serious and professional you really are before they invest their time. Should you offer a fee that is too low you will blow your chances. It's best to research where possible what kind of fees bands can command when playing festivals. We managed to get our starting offers pretty close to what the agent/bands ideally wanted, and by negotiating it once or twice back and forth we started agreeing fees and confirming bands.

It's also important to find out what other plans a band has, especially as we're a small festival – we don't want to end up with the same bands as every other festival, as then the punters would rather go to the more well-known ones and give us a miss.

Our guesses were mainly based on:

- How important the band is to us personally, as one criteria for the line-up is that we only have bands that we like.

- What size venues they play in London/across the country.

- If they have albums/singles coming out towards the festival, which will stir up extra interest.

- How many members in the band.

- We also checked their MySpace to see how many friends/listens/views they've had.

- Where the band will be coming from, for example if they're coming over from the US.

You can put exclusivity clauses in the offer, but we didn't quite know this for our first year and we also believed that as we didn't have a big budget (compared to most other festivals, as we deliberately avoid sponsorship) our offers weren't big enough for us to be able to ask for exclusivity. We have now learnt that it is always worth asking for it, and if the agent/band doesn't agree they will say so, and again it can be negotiated. In our first year, we also ended up paying too much for some of the bands as we didn't quite know what should be a fair fee and found it hard to negotiate with agents who demanded more money.

We found that our personal approach to the bands and showing respect and being personal in the way we worked with the agents made a difference. After all – the agents are helping the bands to realise their dream of being able to make a living from their music, which is something we want to contribute to too, so we don't hold anything against the agents, as seems to be the case with many other promoters/people in the music industry. As we started with no bands confirmed, it helped to have our 'wish list' so that the agents and bands could see what kind of vibe we wanted to create at the festival. And out of all the bands on our original wish list – we actually ended up with a lot of them confirmed and playing at the first ever End of the Road festival. Yay!

## Start marketing

We did advertising, leaflets, flyering, features, previews, reviews in magazines and papers, making sure the bands who were confirmed were doing their bit, which was harder than we thought as we weren't on the ball with getting their PR agents' details when booking, so we have learnt this for 2007. We didn't get a PR agent/officer on board… we only used an online PR company, which is slightly different from someone who would cover absolutely everything.

One of the main marketing tools we used was flyering outside gigs by bands that were playing at the festival, and we also handed out flyers outside other festivals and put our flyers on all the cars in the car parks of other festivals. This was quite a cost-effective way of marketing, as all our dear friends joined in and helped out loads.

It was harder than we thought to get the bands to put the dates up on their websites, do mail-outs, etc… but we have now learnt that as soon as we confirm a band we ask for their PR agent's details, as well as their record label, as they will be in charge of promoting the band, and working together with them will help in promoting the festival too.

## Financing

The story behind the whole financing of the festival is pretty much that Simon sold his house and moved his girlfriend and two kids into rented accommodation, where they are still living now. He also took the profit from his decorating business and put it into the festival, in order to make it the successful event that it turned out. The festival operates on a three-year plan, and made a loss in the first year, which we look at as an investment in the future. Festivals take a lot of work to make a profit, and often make a loss in the first few years.

We are not running the festival to make huge money – it's all about the music, and that's why we are unlikely to grow the capacity of the festival as we want to keep it special and intimate, rather than make it into some kind of money-spinning machine, which seems to be the way for so many other festivals. Even the Green Man festival has now reached a capacity of 10,000.

## MARKETING

This is one area where I was personally too positive – selling 5,000 tickets was much easier said than done, despite an amazing line-up. We ended up spending £40,000 on advertising. We found that the best place to advertise for our type of festival was the *Guardian Guide*. We also took adverts in *Artrocker*, *NME*, *Time Out*, *Mojo*, *Uncut*, *Q* and pretty much anywhere you could think of to do with music.

We also gradually built up contacts with radio stations to get our announcements read out on the news, BBC 6 mainly, who were very supportive. We were lucky to get a list of press contacts from a friend in the industry. Otherwise it is wise to take on a PR agent to help you to get featured as this was also very tricky/hard. We finally took on an online PR agent called Nile-On who helped us get featured on, for example, NME.com, which was one of a few websites that had completely been ignoring us until we confirmed Ryan Adams. Make sure the festival is listed *everywhere*, such as Virtual Festivals, Efestivals, etc.

Start building a mailing list as soon as you can. This needs to be a proper mailing list – not a personal address book on Outlook, Yahoo or similar, as it has the potential of growing to thousands, and you will need to be able to do mass mails with no problem.

## Selling tickets

Starting selling tickets is important for cash flow, unless you've got a big backer as the bigger bands often want 50 per cent in advance. We sold the tickets from our website, just like we are doing now – you can check here: www.endoftheroadfestival.com. We had to find a company to create the interface, so that the actual ticket sales and where the ticket buyers enter their personal information takes place on a secure server. There are a lot of companies around who do this, and we were lucky to be recommended Turtle by the lovely people who run Blissfields (another small festival). But as we got closer to the time of the festival, and we needed to reach out to more potential ticket buyers, we had to go with Ticket Master and Ticket Web, as they have huge databases that they market their events to.

The problem with ticket agents is that you won't get your money until after the event, so we had to limit the number of tickets they were selling on our behalf. One of the benefits of using someone like Ticket Master was that they printed our tickets for us, as this can be a tricky business as you don't want the tickets to be easy to forge. By having hardcopy tickets, you can also start selling through record shops, etc. Rough Trade Records were very helpful and sold our tickets for us in their shops in London.

## Taking on someone to look after your food/non-food stalls applications

It is important to work with someone who knows what it is you want, and we were recommended Jo Rogers by the guys at Ashton Court festival, and Jo did a brilliant job in 2006. Not only does the market manager need to find the kind of caterers that you want, but also make sure that the caterers follow all the rules. Please have a look at the application forms for this year to get an idea of what info is required, it's mainly risk assessments and Health & Safety, which are important factors from an event management point of view. From our personal point of view, we really care about the environment and organic/ethical products. See www.endoftheroadfestival.com (look under the Contacts section, scroll down to the Catering/Market section).

At festivals you need to provide roughly one food stall per 1,000 people... but as we *love* food and wanted everybody to have a good selection of caterers, we probably doubled this. We simply wrote down a list of the kind of food that we wanted at the festival, and then asked Jo to come up with a shortlist based on the applications. Caterers would find our application details on the website and Jo also had a massive mailing list of caterers that she has worked with on past events.

## Get quotes from all contractors

The list of contractors involved in a festival is long: toilets, showers, water, stages, lighting, electrics, plumber, waste, recycling, fencing, tents, pa, sound, stewards, backline, security, transport vehicles on site, site crew, stage managers, staff catering, artist catering, bars, marquees, projectors/cinema, riders for the artists and so on (usually the job for a production manager). Well, if you get a production manager on board early – they will do all this for you! And it will be much quicker for them, as they are likely to already have a team of suppliers and contractors who they use over and over again, depending on how long they've been in the business.

It is a pretty big job, and we spent about four to seven months approaching contractors for quotes and then negotiating the quotes. It was hard to know what was a decent price as we had never done this before, so Steve Hunt was very helpful giving us advice along the way, and then as soon as we took on our production manager (only two months before the festival was taking place), he pretty much got a load of new quotes from all the contractors we had been in touch with and also from his own preferred suppliers, and then weighed up the cost against quality, as it's not always such a good idea to go for the cheapest quote.

## Start confirming contractors

I think Chris based his decisions firstly on if a quote fitted into our budget, then on the experience and reputation of the company within their field, then on if he knew them personally and liked working with them. Some companies would be based far away from the festival site, and some would be preferred on the basis that they were based locally… but it all depends on which services you're looking at, and you need someone with experience to help you with this.

You must have a production manager in place by the time you go on site, at the very, very latest, as they will be making sure that the logistics of building the site run smoothly and to time together with the site manager.

See above, we only took on our production manager two months before the festival actually took place, which really was the very last minute. In our second year, we have taken on Chris straight after the first festival finished, in order to let him work on the licence, the contractors, etc from the start and much more in advance compared to last year.

## Licensing authority inspection before being allowed to open

I personally wasn't there unfortunately, as I was working on the bands and artist liaison aspects of the festival into the very last minute and only arrived the day before the festival. My job during the festival itself was to head up the artist liaison team, which was a great job – but very stressful and it meant pretty much working throughout the whole festival. Simon was on site almost from the very start of the build-up and on the day of the inspection, unfortunately, a lot of the items for inspection were not in place, such as for example fire extinguishers. So, there was a lot of running around and organising for Simon and Chris to make sure that everything complied by the check the next day. During the meeting with the licensing authority after the festival, to discuss improvements, etc, this was one of the main points that they were not happy with. On the inspection – everything should be completely in order.

## Open to the public, run the festival – wohooo!!! (how we felt)

Amazing! Personally, I was then really really busy meeting and greeting bands, making sure that their riders were in their dressing rooms, that everybody arrived on time, got on stage on time, found the stage they were meant to be on, and were happy and enjoying themselves! For the festival in whole (three stages), we had an artist liaison team of eight people, including myself. This was a little too few – but we managed to do it by working long hours and keeping each other smiley and happy. For this kind of role, you need people/friends who you can trust and rely on and who won't get starstruck.

## Closing

Close the site to the public after the event, clean up, clear up and follow up with reviews, feedback from festival goers and so on… We had a festival questionnaire that we asked festival goers to fill in while at the festival and then we also sent it out afterwards, and the feedback was absolutely amazing! And people really made an effort to come up with ideas for improvements and share their thoughts with us, which we really appreciate and we have implemented some of the ideas for 2007.

I was knackered after having worked three very long days, and left the site together with my mum, brother and my friends on the Monday, after helping people to get on buses to the train stations and getting taxis for those in a rush, etc. Simon, together with some of his family and friends, stayed on site and helped the site crew with the take-down, lost property, litter picking and all those lovely things that needs doing to return the site to its former glory. There were reviews in quite a few papers and magazines, and especially online, which we were so grateful for, as most people had an amazing time and the *Independent* called it an 'artistic triumph' – wohooo!

We thought of writing a thankyou list and publishing it on our website after the event, as our hearts were so full of love for everybody and anybody that had contributed to the festival in one way or another… but this list would have had hundreds of names on it and you always worry that you might miss someone off… but we are forever grateful!

And just about a month or two after it all took place, the End of the Road festival went on to win the award for Best New Festival in the UK Festival Awards 2006, which was totally unexpected and yet another amazing experience – especially with the competition from so many other new Boutique festivals. And at the award ceremony we got to thank some of our fantastic team such as Chris, Ben, Philip, Carly, Jennifer, Molly, Luke, Simon, Steve, Jenny, Jo, Cat, Jason, Adam, Kenny, Ro and all our friends and family who helped make this dream come true.

## IN CONCLUSION

And there we are. Many of you are going to be thinking and feeling like this when you start up your own ventures. I thought it was only right to keep the sentiments written by Sofia to show you are not alone and that dreams still can be achieved. You will start out inexperienced and doubtful but you can break through those barriers by just simply getting on and doing it. These guys have proved it. I liked the story and I'm happy to give the team a platform to show the world how it can be done. Make no mistake though, this took a whole lot of guts and great financial risk. How many of us really would sell our houses or would have the family and friends in our lives to back us up and go for it?

Setting up a festival is a huge job. I think you are looking at a ball park figure for a very small festival of £100,000 and upwards to really get it done properly. To do all of this and still keep your integrity is a testament to the passion and love for music that the End of the Road team have. My friends, dreams can be achieved, despite the odds, never ever let anyone tell you otherwise.

# Music Law and Legal Advice

I decided for this chapter to enlist the services of a music industry lawyer. Elliot Chalmers from www.musiclawadvice.co.uk is an independent music industry solicitor with the same street spirit as ourselves at The Rock and Roll Times. I realised it would be worth you reading the information straight from the horse's mouth. Having legal representation will be one of the big issues all artists will have to deal with. So I'm happy to hand you over to the legal guy.

## MUSIC ADVICE

The role of a lawyer can be paramount to a band in the minefield that is the music industry. They will look after you and protect you from exploitation and ideally make sure you are left to focus on the creation of music. There are still bands out there who think there is no harm in signing contracts without any advice because they are naive or believe the goodwill they have in themselves will extend to business agreements. But things can turn sour quickly and often to the detriment of the band's existence. An industry qualified legal adviser should always look at every single contract that is ever offered to you.

When I set up as an independent music law adviser I looked at the way law firms operated and treated music clients. Admittedly, five years ago the music industry was drastically different to what we see today, to the point that a book like this would not have been possible or needed. An unsigned band back then would have had a shelf life of around a year and were unlikely to be offered any kind of deal until a major or indie label showed interest. If that deal didn't come about then unless they had outside investment they would most likely give up the ghost. Now of course unsigned bands are likely to be offered numerous types of contracts before a major record or management deal comes along, ranging from digital to production to distribution.

## LAWYER'S ROLE AND DUTIES

### What to expect from legal advice

Many law firms charge a standard hourly rate of anything from £200 to £300 so it can be pricey, as looking over a contract can take them around eight hours. You may often find that a trainee does the work instead of a senior lawyer. That's not to say it isn't always worth it, but for a new band it can be beneficial to find someone like myself that does not charge an hourly rate and is your sole point of contact. Always make sure that you understand the rates and what you are actually getting. Never allow a lawyer to blind you with legal jargon when doing work for you. It is their responsibility to explain and justify their work to you so you should make sure you know what they are doing.

### What you actually need

You will need anything from general advice to specific work such as contracts, band agreements and help with copyrights and registration of songs. It can always help just to get an idea of what you should be doing and thinking about. For instance, copyright and artists' rights can be quite complicated (see later) so it can be beneficial to have this explained to you. I get a lot of enquiries from people asking for representation who have read that a lawyer can get you a deal. There's no doubt that larger law firms do have contacts with labels and publishers, but this does not mean they can guarantee anything. So never rely solely on this or commit to anyone on the back of a contact they might have. I will always try and recommend bands to my contacts, but will not boost their expectations by making unrealistic promises.

The other thing about legal advice is that it's not always absolute. The client has every right to question the lawyer's judgment and suggest alternative ways of doing things. This can mean you get more out of them as well as giving you a better insight into the situation. The artist should work with the lawyer in the same way you would work with a label or management company – have an input and make it clear what your plans and expectations are.

## COPYRIGHT ADVICE

One of the most common issues I have to deal with concerns the subject of copyright. Many artists aren't fully aware of what constitutes copyright and more importantly what the right actually means or entitles them to. This lack of knowledge can lead to potential infringements and situations that can seriously damage the artist.

## Sound recordings

One of the most important concepts which need to be grasped is that there is a copyright in a sound recording, which is quite separate and distinct from the copyright in the song which has been recorded, and these separate copyrights can be owned by different people. For example, Elton John writes a song. Marilyn Manson wants to make a recording of that song! Elton owns the copyright in the song, but Marilyn will own the copyright in the recording once he has obtained Elton's permission or 'licence' in order to be able to record it. It means that Elton would have to ask Marilyn if he then wants to ever perform the song. In the real world, Elton is a songwriter under contract to a publisher and is signed to a record company, so the likelihood is that the publishing company will own the copyright in his song. The record company will own the separate copyright in the recording and will have to obtain a licence from the publishers so that Marilyn can record Elton's song and his label can release it! His label will have to pay a 'copyright' or 'mechanical' royalty to the publishers for the privilege of using Elton's song, and the publishers will in turn pay part of that royalty to him, the original writer. This means that several parties will be involved once a song is written and performed so it is vital to be aware of all the different strands that make up the rights in a song.

## How can you protect your works?

The procedures for copyright protection in the UK are far less straightforward as there is no official register that is approved by English law. There is no central copyright index, or forms to fill in. A composer secures copyright automatically as a direct result of having created a new work. It must, however, be original. If you copy or adapt someone else's song without permission, in whole or part, you will not acquire any copyright of your own. Instead this would be seen as an infringement and the original copyright owner will be able to take legal action against you.

Without an official register it may be less costly to own your copyright, but it also gives more opportunity to those that may want to use a song illegally. A situation can arise in which more people could claim that a song is owned by them and even attempt to use or adapt that song for their own purposes. I have had clients who have heard a song on the radio or in a record shop and have recognised either a riff or a part that is incredibly familiar. If they can prove that it was originally produced by them then they will have a potential case and will be able to take further action, no matter how small the part was. The problems begin though when you have to ask yourself whether it is a genuine composition that is simply exactly the same as another track or whether it is an actual direct infringement.

Due to the lack of a one-off register various methods of protection have evolved over the years as music has become more and more lucrative. Some of the more popular methods are shown below.

- Posting copies of your work to yourselves in a sealed registered envelope, obtaining a stamped dated post office receipt, and keeping the unopened envelope and receipt in a safe place in case they are ever required for evidential purposes.

- Depositing a copy of your work with a lawyer, accountant or other reputable professional in return for a dated receipt.

These measures are helpful in recording that the work was in existence on a particular date, but they are not a guarantee of copyright ownership as they are always open to possible tampering or copying.

## What does copyright protection provide?

If you are the owner of a copyright, e.g. in a song, then unless you have given permission for any of these specific activities, no one else can do any of the following with your song:

- copy it
- issue copies to the public
- perform or play it in public
- broadcast it or include it in a cable programme service
- make an adaptation of it.

## How long does copyright last?

Musical works are protected by copyright until 70 years after the end of the calendar year in which the author died. After that, they fall into the public domain, which means that anyone can record or perform them without paying the original copyright owner. Copy in a sound recording generally expires 50 years from the end of the calendar year of first release, or in the case of an unreleased sound recording, 50 years from the end of the year in which it was made.

## Advice

There is no doubt that understanding your copyright position will go a long way to helping you understand any music contracts that you might be offered. When being advised on a recording deal you will have a much clearer picture of why a record company or publishing house demand that you assign certain rights to them. This will allow you to be fully aware of your rights throughout the contract period, and to know what those rights mean and how they are being used. You don't need to understand all aspects of a contract, but I have found that giving artists some extra knowledge is likely to put off less genuine companies from offering you an unfair or unacceptable deal.

## IN CONCLUSION

OK, I'm back. This is a chapter that really could have gotten too complicated and far too boring with technical detail and I think as long as you follow the basics you will be on safe ground. With digital recordings it's hard to get ripped off these days as it's a lot easier to prove who wrote a song and when. A lot of music law is archaic and is a throw-back to a much darker time when the sharks really did run the show. The music industry has become a lot more professional and it's only really dumb stupid people who try to rip people off. So the likelihood of your super digital recording getting ripped off by someone else is remote. Nevertheless, follow the basics and always keep one open eye. We're off to never never land...

# Keeping Your Accounts

## RED TAPE

Let's face it. Tax, accounts and book-keeping are all very boring. When I think of these things my eyes glaze over. And to be honest the only glaze I want to see is on my doughnuts. Krispy Kremes please. Actually I can't eat the old Kremes anymore. Not since I overdosed on them. Thanks honey! But I'm afraid it's a subject that needs to be taken care of otherwise you will find yourself in trouble somewhere down the road. Tax and accounts is a very specialised subject so you will need to employ a music industry accountant. Because there is no way in hell I could do this subject any kind of justice. I'd be trapped in technical hell and I don't deserve that, do I? The rules when it comes to tax seem to change on a regular basis and it seems the Inland Revenue wolves are modernising their department to be more user friendly to you, the people. Even if they are just another archaic governmental department using smoke and mirrors to relieve you of your money.

## The basics

I'm only going to highlight a very few basics and what you are entitled to claim for.

- There are the basic costs most bands will suffer. And even then it's only really to get you thinking professionally about keeping some basic form of book-keeping.

- The rest is a case of you calling a nice friendly accountant and employing them.

Make no mistake though, as a business you will have to be legit. I know a few bands who have been tracked down by the tax man and nailed to the cross. Pleading ignorance is not going to work. And whilst most bands will run at a loss, at least initially, it's best to keep your dealings in some kind of order. When you have set up your label or the band is creating income then you should either have told the Inland Revenue or be about to. If you have serious intentions about creating and sustaining a career in music then the only option is to play safe and do everything a legitimate business is supposed to do. I mentioned earlier about bands being caught out by the taxman. Well, when it comes to the Inland Revenue investigating bands, they simply get lists from all the venues across the UK and decide who to go after. If you are not on their register and they check your websites out and see you are selling CDs and merch then you can expect a knock on the door. And you will have no excuse outside of death to justify why you have been very naughty indeed.

So keep receipts for every single expense. Where possible, pay for as much as you can with a credit/debit card. That way you have a receipt upon payment and an electronic one when it comes to your statements. This will help with any problems with claims, should any arise.

## Business accounts

You will need a separate business account as it will get very messy if you have a personal account running all your business transactions. I know when you have a business account you get stiffed on costs, etc, but bank costs linked to business accounts can be deducted or at least off-set against expenses.

## EXPENSES

A small summary of things you can claim expenses for. A word of caution though. This is not a complete guide by any means and is for educational purposes only. I don't want the UK taxman knocking on my door kicking my arse because you told him it was my fault you're now in the clink for tax evasion. (Well, you may get a slap on the wrist.) It's just to give you a basic understanding, ok...

When it comes to what you can claim for, these are guidelines. For some you will be able to claim 100 per cent and for some a fraction. You will need to prove to the taxman that they are directly related to your business. Again, your accountant will advise you on the complete breakdown.

## Rehearsal rooms

This one is an expense most bands will accumulate a lot over the space of a month. So try and get receipts all the time. Over the space of a year this can amount to a fair few hundred quid. Most bands will rehearse at least once a week and some three or four times a week.

## Recording studios

This can be one of the biggest costs accrued by an artist. Any time you enter a studio you know full well it's not going to be cheap. If it all works out and you start selling CDs then you off-set the initial costs against expenses.

## Stage clothes

Clothes that are used to wear on stage should be 100 per cent reclaimable. But unless you dress like Kiss it may be difficult to get the Levis through. Still, you are entitled so keep records of everything you buy for stage wear. Platform boots ain't cheap!

## Travel

When you are on a tour travelling from one town to the next you may be able to claim back the costs. It becomes a bit difficult to argue if you are playing the same venue week in week out, but outside of that you should get expenses back. Touring especially comes under that umbrella as you will be able to prove the distance and mileage. Keep a log book for this as it will help you when it comes to justifying why you are claiming.

## Overnight accommodation

As a band you will spend a fair bit of time away from home. If you are not stuck on a tour bus or on a mate's floor you may be able to claim for hotel accommodation and meals.

## Instruments

As instruments are the tools of your trade they fall under the expense of running a business. This includes insurance, any repairs and replacement of strings, drumsticks, mic stands and any form of audio equipment you need to do the job.

## Press promotion

Any kind of paid advertising, publicity material like pictures, posters, badges or any item with your band name displayed is applicable.

## Commissions

This includes fees paid out to managers, agents, solicitors and accountants. As these are professional services rendered to you to run the business they are accepted.

## Stationery

All matter of running an office is claimable. Telephone costs may be argued but if you have a business line it simplifies matters. Same with your mobile phone, you may only be able to claim for a percentage if you use your phones for business and pleasure.

## Postage

Any time you post out a CD or T-shirt or any kind of band mail you will need a post office receipt. This can get expensive also. So, each time you visit the post office get into the frame of mind where you enter the receipt and who it was posted to in an account program like Excel. It will save you the hassle of sitting down at the end of the month with 200 receipts trying to figure out where everything went.

## Bank charges

A business account will be needed to keep everything nice and simple. Any charges from this account can be expensed back to running the business.

## KEEPING TRACK

So not a huge list but enough to get you thinking. A lot of those claims generally would not be thought about from a band's point of view. How many of you actually get receipts from your local rehearsal studio? Or how many times have you posted a CD to a fan and not retained the costs? It's the little things that start to add up. I did speak to a few accountants but, to be frank, it didn't make good reading. It's a very specialised subject and one best left to the experts. Getting hold of a definitive and detailed breakdown of what musicians are entitled to proved difficult as a lot of cases can boil down to having to show the taxman why you need those things. And quite frankly it's boring as hell. Have you ever read an account manual? Forget it.

The best thing you can do is create an Excel spreadsheet and start to input expenses as and when you get them. Even a good old fashioned notebook and pen will do the trick as long as you have good handwriting. This is definitely the one area where you will need to play by the rules.

A good accountant will be able to advise you on exactly everything you need to be aware of and what you can claim back against expenses. They will advise you on the best way to conduct your employment status and guide you through any minefields. It's what you will be paying them for. www.hmrc.gov.uk has all the information you need to start up as self-employed. As for the rest, get a good music industry accountant on board. Because life isn't long enough to read though all the crap they throw at you...see you later!

# Seeking Funding

For most of you the best way to seek funding is to apply to the Arts Council/National Lottery. I've known bands and individuals receive up to £10,000 and whilst the process is slightly tedious it's worth applying. The website is www.artscouncil.org.uk/funding/ where you will find the forms you need to get the process started. There will be a 26-odd page fact sheet that tells you of the requirements and explains the procedure. Go easy at this stage as there is a lot of information to digest. They also have contact numbers to call an adviser on and it's worth calling them up to discuss your grant proposal. The application form is in PDF format and you will be required to write an additional proposal in Word detailing what it is you are applying for. I've helped bands seek funding for recording CDs and press and promotion.

## WHAT YOU CAN APPLY FOR

There is no real limit to what you can apply for as most areas related to music are covered. For instance, there is even a section for touring and maintenance of vehicles. What you need to do is take your time and don't rush. Around 80 per cent of applications get rejected due to people rushing them and not filling them in correctly. It's like going shopping when you are hungry. It's not till you get home you realise you've bought nothing but chocolate and junk food.

Whatever area you are applying for make sure you detail every-thing. Let's say you are looking at pressing your CD. We can assume you have already paid the recording costs (as they do expect you to have raised finance for certain areas already) and you are now ready to press 1,000 CDs. You would need three independent quotes from three companies. I have enclosed a real live template of the kind of proposal you will be expected to write and I think it would give you an understanding of how to approach it. The questions you read are the same ones you will face. The answers are my own, but will help you understand what you will need to say. I would advise you to use your own style, words, and figures and to just adapt what I have shown here. It's for educational purposes only!

## 1 You and your work

*(Insert band name) are a hard rock band with a diverse style that incorporates a hard sound, a tight groove and dynamic melodies. We have recorded our debut album at a cost of £5,000 which we raised ourselves through selling copies of our first EP. The next stage in the band's development is to press, promote, distribute and sell the album. This is a critical time for the band as our EP was acclaimed through the music press, including underground and internet music sites, local and national newspapers and music magazines. Our debut video featured on national TV including Kerrang and Scuzz, enabling the band to build its fan base and secure bigger gigs to play and increase our touring boundaries.*

*We plan to press and duplicate the debut album to a print run of 5,000 initial copies. Included in the cost of £5,000 we require to do this are PR costs. We aim to secure three independent quotes from pressing companies to ensure we get the best deal. In order to market and promote the album to its fullest we have enlisted a music industry specialist who will help us in all stages of the campaign.*

*The plan we have so far is to secure the funding with the best deal available and then in this order:*

- *Gigs: We plan to do a run of 50 dates around the UK.*

- *Press: in each town we play we will target the local newspaper.*

- *University press and radio.*

- *Internet music magazines and webzines.*

- *National music magazines and newspapers.*

- *Along with national TV rotating our second video on the relevant music channels.*

*We are in talks with Kerrang and Scuzz amongst others to play the video to coincide with the release of the first single.*

*What we would like to achieve with this activity is for the band to become self-sufficient and make a living playing the music we love. We also have plans in place to ensure we are able to record the second album when the time comes. Also, this is about being able to do this for ourselves, but we are always open to the opportunity that a record label will sign the band and we can get to a vastly more professional level. At present all band members work full time so we spend all our remaining time writing, rehearsing, gigging and focusing on the music and the band. This does limit us from a financial and time point of view. But we believe that we have a fan base we can add to that would bring great value to not only our lives but our music.*

*The band means everything to its members and we always aim for the highest professional standards. Something as important as a debut album release means we cannot even consider anything less than we ourselves put in. Be it time, money or love. We are willing to work with like-minded people who have our band's dreams at heart to enable us to play our music.*

## 2 Making it happen

*The debut album is fully completed and now needs to be released commercially. We have a fan base that we know will buy the album and from the gigs we have played this year we have added and continue to add new fans. In total we have played around 40 gigs this year to an audience of over 2,000–3,000. As an unsigned band at the touring level we play we hope to keep adding to that figure.*

*The first part of the campaign was to get three independent quotes from CD pressing companies for a print run of 5,000 CDs. This includes the complete package of the CD itself, with art work, inlays, CD cases, barcodes and delivery.*

▶

*We have set up an online shop via our website to sell the CD to fans which will include Paypal facilities and secure banking.*

*We are constantly playing gigs so we aim to sell the CD ourselves.*

*A press campaign targeting the towns we play will ensure the publicity we need, which includes magazines and newspapers, university press and radio, internet webzines. Our video will be played on relevant music shows in conjuction with the release of the album, gigs and press campaign. We are getting the album onto iTunes and other online digital record stores that will have a worldwide presence.*

*With the level of publicity in conjunction with live dates we hope to sell the initial 5,000 print run to enable us to press more and continue with developments to our second album. We have a mailing list of 1,000 fans who continually ask us when the album will be released. We know we can start the campaign strong and capitalise on that.*

## 3 Your budget

*So far the band's costs extend to £5,000 for the cost of recording the album. We financed this ourselves. The next stage is getting the CD into the public domain and to do this we need financial help. Below are three independent quotes from CD pressing companies for units of 1,000, 3,000 and 5,000 CDs. It's imperative to the future of the band that we are able to sell the CD online and in the shops and gigs to help us progress further. We are asking for a further £5,000 to help with the costs below.*

### Quote number 1

*Pressing company number 1*

*1,000 = £709.50 + VAT £833.66 inc VAT*

*3,000 = £1,425.00 + VAT £1,674.38 inc VAT*

*5,000 = £2,116.70 + VAT £2,487.12 inc VAT*

*The extra 2p cost for litho print on the disc would only take effect on the 1,000 unit quantity, not on the 3,000 and 5,000 unit price.*

*Quote number 2*

*Pressing company number 2*

*1,000*

*Glass-mastering – £0 – free*

*CD inc five-colour\* onbody print – 40p × 1,000 = £400*

*Jewel case/black tray @ 14p × 1,000 = £140*

*4pp booklet 4/1 + inlay 4/0 @ 11p = £110*

*Cello-wrapping – free*

*Delivery to one UK address – free*

*Setup:*

*CD label – 4 × £8 – £32*

*Booklet/inlay – 9 × £8 – £72*

*Total: £754+ VAT (£885.95)*

*Prices exc VAT @ 17.5%*

*\* CMYK print onto white base – screen print can be up to four pantone colours on a white base or CMYK.*

*Turnaround – seven to ten working days*

*Allow for up to ten per cent overs/unders – you pay for the exact number received*

| Quantity | 500 | 1,000 | 3,000 | 5,000 |
|---|---|---|---|---|
| Glassmastering | £220 | free | free | free |
| CD | 44p | 40p | 37p | 36p |
| Jewel case | 14p | 14p | 14p | 14p |
| Booklet/inlay set | 22p | 11p | 11p | 9p |
| Total: £1.24 | (£620) | 65p(£650) | 62p(£1,860) | 58.5p(£2,925) |

### Quote number 3

*Pressing company number 3*

| Item | Unit price | Quantity | Total | Total inc VAT |
|---|---|---|---|---|
| CD replication with full colour screen print. Jewel case +8pp 4/4 book+inlay 4/0 | £0.61 | 1,000 | £610.00 | £716.75 |
| CD replication with full colour screen print. Jewel case +8pp 4/4 book+inlay 4/0 | £0.54 | 3,000 | £1,620.00 | £1,903.50 |
| CD replication with full colour screen print. Jewel case +8pp 4/4 book+inlay 4/0 | £0.53 | 5,000 | £2,650.00 | £3,113.75 |
| Overnight delivery | TBC | TBC | TBC | TBC |

*Other costs will be for*

*Postage*

*Telephone*

*Application fees for music industry bodies like PRS, MCPS, Song Writers and Composers' Association.*

*The CD pressing for us is great value for money as we will be able to reinvest in the band and continue its development. Also, it will enable us to finance the second album and continue our career. Without the finance for the pressing, it would leave us between a rock and a hard place. So, value-wise, with the three independent quotes we have had, it is the best value we can hope for.*

*We aim to sell our CD digitally online to help with the costs to fund further CD pressing and merchandise. Also, we will get the album onto other online digital record labels to help us further. Any money we make through gigs always goes on expenses to make the gigs possible. So the online digital sales will be a valuable part of the campaign.*

*Our manager will ensure that financial controls are in place. Each penny spent will be documented and accounted for. Also, we would have a monthly financial forecast in place for the outlay and then for the sales of the CDs. Our manager has been in control of company-wide budgets for most of his professional career so we are able to utilise his experience and make sure the money is spent wisely on the band for the betterment of our careers.*

*We are asking for the full amount as we invested all we could to make the best sounding album we could. Taking into consideration the very high level of professionalism needed in today's oversaturated market, we simply had to do the best job we could. And we are very proud of the end result. Our aim is to become self-sufficient and with the aid of a grant and the management we have in place to make the best decisions based on experience, we know we stand a very good chance of becoming self-sufficient. The album is ready for release now and it could take months, perhaps longer than a year, for us to raise again the amount of finance we need to release the CD.*

### 4 Benefit to you and the public

*This would be the best benefit that the band could have in terms of being able to release, market and promote our debut album. It would enable us to continue with the band's career in a very real and positive way as opposed to continue having to scrimp and save, starve and spend longer than is worthwhile to give our music a platform and showcase our songs. It would get us into the wider musical arena, not only in the UK but the wider world in general and give us a real shot at being successful. The band is at a critical point in its career and this would give us the credibility, not just for ourselves as people but as musicians and songwriters.*

*The benefit it would give to the public is a chance for our fan base to hear the album and for us to build and continue building a bigger fan base. Touring, promoting and marketing an album is a constant process and the release of the album would be UK-wide ensuring it's in the public domain for fans of rock music to hear. When we play gigs the one constant question we have always had is 'When will you release an album?' We know there is an audience for our style of music that isn't being serviced with the current policies of the music industry, which includes the record companies, Radio 1, MTV, etc. We have shown through hard work, belief and hard core determination and against all the odds thrown at us, that when we play we always make new fans.*

▶

*We aim to reach the public through a press and marketing campaign along with touring. The press campaign is being orchestrated by our manager. It is as follows.*

- *Press and PR in all major university towns in UK.*

- *Local and national press exposure.*

- *Websites and underground campaigns.*

- *National music-based magazines and fanzines.*

- *Placement of our video on Kerrang TV, Scuzz TV along with other relevant music TV programmes.*

- *Touring extensively throughout the UK in support of the album.*

*The campaign will be executed by our manager who has a 15-year background in press and publicity. It's been part of the management's job in the music industry to create UK-wide profiles for bands and companies.*

*Rock music worldwide has always been strong. And 2007 is no different. We know through touring the UK, with hits on both our website and MySpace, that we have lots of interest from fans and people wanting to see us and hear our music. From our early days we have been chosen to play festivals, record early demos and build a strong fan base from very frugal beginnings. Over time we came to realise that we had music and songs we could make something of and that people kept coming to see us and request recorded music. We have grown the band to a point where it's become semi-professional despite a lack of finance. More importantly we have belief in what we are doing and have created a place for ourselves in the marketplace where we can now maximise our potential. We just need that little bit of extra help to get there.*

### 5 Meeting our ambitions for the arts

*The influx of the grant from The Arts Council would definitely enable our band (insert band name) to thrive. This would give us the power to determine our own strategies, plan our growth and continue to build our career from a self-sufficient point of view. Through prudent planning and execution of the grant we can control events and invest in our future endeavours.*

*It basically means we get the chance to exist in what is a very cut-throat market with a good chance, through creative thinking, of being able to compete with bands who are signed to record labels with big budgets. The grant would help us run the band as a business, as well as continue making music, but to intelligently consider the influences and constraints outside of our control and give us a fighting chance to create long-term goals.*

*It also means we can get our music to like-minded people. From research given to us by our manager, for every band that is signed and becomes successful, there are hundreds that don't get that chance. Digital technology and the internet has now given bands like us a chance to expose our music to an appreciative audience. We would run the band like it was already signed to a record label. With everything from the songs, to management, PR, accounts and further investment in the band we can be as effective as possible.*

*All in all, the help of the grant would be a life saver for us. We would make sure we continued to do the best we can. As we have always done. It should be stated that we have been involved with people who have offered to help us but have turned out to do the opposite. We have come a long way with this band, and we remain focused, determined, believing in our music and have hope for our futures. With the support of the Arts Council, the grant would free us to create and release the music we all believe in.*

### 6 Evaluation

*How we propose to evaluate: the evaluation process would consist of continuing to seek the best deals for further pressing versus the initial run. We would continue to find the best way to sell our CDs and incorporate any new information into future planning and strategies. Month by month we will be reviewing the press campaign versus the album sales to find better ways to enable us to make the most of any opportunity that may present itself. We will keep an activity report on the band campaign and readjust requirements when or if necessary. All decisions will be made in regards to financial, business and creative sense.*

So, that's more or less the process you will have to go through. I've included it to save you some time and a lot of headaches when you get to the time when you apply. Like I said, your own individual project will more or less write itself but it's a useful template. When you have finished writing yours, call up the Arts Council and ask if there is someone you can email your application to for perusal. They will advise you along each step you need to take.

## OTHER IDEAS

### PRS Foundation

The PRS Foundation is another source to tap into. They have grants available up to £3,000 and for the application process along with a step-by-step guide to follow visit www.prsfoundation.co.uk. There is a detailed section that advises you in all you need to do.

Lastly, never underestimate asking friends or family for any source of finance. If you do this it's worth drawing up a plan with a timetable of events and timelines. This is being professional and may avoid any kind of trouble later on. Normally I would never advise anyone to borrow money from friend or family, but as I've seen bands do it and prove successful it is worth considering. Local businesses are also starting to get in on the act of financing bands/artists as they see a potential return on the initial loan. It should go without saying now that of course you need to get legal advice before you do this. Again, it's still a place some bands wouldn't dream of tapping into and it can prove to be a worthwhile venture. Always keep an eye open for any kind of opportunity.

Seeking funding is down to individual belief and the tenacity to follow through. You could spend hours on the internet researching potential grant organisations and at some point you may strike pay dirt. Your individual circumstances will always affect what you are entitled to and how hard or easy it is to attain a grant. But like everything else in this life, only by daring to succeed will you indeed succeed. Good luck!

# Music Industry Events

## IN THE CITY

www.inthecity.co.uk

In the City is the annual UK music convention. Bigwigs from the music industry, both UK and USA, descend on Manchester every year to talk about and normally cry into their favourite alcoholic beverage over the state of the music industry and how digital downloads are killing them. The event is mainly for music industry personnel and isn't really open to the public. (The gigs are though.) It's a ticket event only. Around 60 bands are chosen to play where the cream of the A&R crop, who mostly already know who the bands are, will run up and down Manchester catching as many bands as they can. The event is worth playing for the experience, but don't go thinking because there's so many A&R in attendance it will get you a deal. It won't. There is an application process which is listed on the ITC website every summer ready for the event itself in October time. You will be requested to submit your CD and then you will hear back if you are successful or not.

Every CD is played by a good team of people so your music will get a good listen. Something else to think about from your campaign perspective is that there will loads of press people checking out the coolest bands, where you may well get some good reviews and a slight buzz out of it. Also, the successful bands are listed on the website so as the word spreads you will get all sorts of people checking out your band by virtue of being listed by ITC. Keep an eye out in the music press and check the ITC website to see when the application process is open.

The best of In the City is held in London where the four best bands play to a full venue of music industry people. If you get to that stage you've done OK. But again, it's no guarantee of a record deal. So look at it as a chance to get more exposure for your campaign and above all, enjoy it.

## GO NORTH

Go North was launched in 2001 so acts/bands from Northern Scotland, the Highlands and Islands could showcase in front of music industry and media representatives on their own patch. It became obvious that bands further up north were finding it impossible to jump in the back of a van for a 12-hour drive to head to London to play the Bull and Gate in Kentish Town to three people before jumping back in the van to head home. Go North was created to get the UK music industry (all London-based) to head to Scotland. The good thing about this event it that it really does help young bands get access to music industry professionals using seminars and Q&A sessions aimed at helping emerging artists, managers and labels.

Traditionally held in several venues in Aberdeen's Belmont Street, Go North has become the largest newcomer festival in Scotland with over 60 bands playing over two nights in 2006. Again, the way this differs from ITC is that these gigs are free to the public with the seminars aimed at the bands and young professionals. This is the kind of setup I would endorse because the industry are there to see bands. The event has grown with several locations including Aberdeen, Dundee, Inverness and even Moscow added to the calendar. It's good to have professionals sit on a panel for the kids to ask any question they can think of. It does create a buzz and the event is worthwhile. It's open to bands/artists who live in that part of the world so if you live in Plymouth you don't qualify. But that's the nature of the beast. Bands in England have had it lucky when it's come to industry exposure and I'm sure with time an organisation will be set to cover bands on the south coast.

If you are a Scottish band go to **www.goevents.org** for the application process.

# BELFEST

The Belfest is a similar, if older, operation to Go North. Set in the University district of Belfast it's a great chance for Northern Ireland's finest to get exposure to the UK A&R hooligans. Again, there are seminars where you can sit in and find out what record labels think and ask all the questions you like. Set up in conjunction with Nimic (Northern Ireland Music Industry Commission) it's funded and professionally organised to look after the interests of young bands and artists as well as young industry professionals looking to break into the business side of music. You have to be based in Northern Ireland, so have a look at **www.belfest.com** to see how you can get onto the next event.

I think in the future you will start seeing a lot more of these events around the entire UK as people and organisations start seeing their merits. The public can get into the gigs for free and the bands get exposure to the industry, so as I see it everyone can get something from it. The seminar programme includes topics like:

- managing your career
- doing it for yourself in the music industry
- marketing in the digital world
- sales and distribution.

Amongst other things, the aim is to get young bands and managers into thinking how they should develop their careers, creating an infrastructure along the exact same lines as I'm telling you in this book. Not only that, you get to hang out in a very cool district of Belfast with some of the nicest people in the world!

# WELSH MUSIC FOUNDATION

The Welsh Music Foundation (**www.welshmusicfoundation. com**) is a website and resource portal set up to help in the development of the music industry in Wales. This site is a great place for young bands looking at understanding the music industry. It organises events and seminars similar to the ones already mentioned along with business start-up advice and guidance. The website has a music industry directory along with information on music-based educational courses. Anyone with an interest in getting involved in music, from a band perspective, management, PR, promoting, etc should look at the directory section for articles and help sections. Again, another example of a particular area of the UK getting itself organised to help out people around their own region.

## SOUTH BY SOUTH WEST

www.sxsw.com

South By South West is the big one. Held in Austin, Texas this event is probably out of reach for most unsigned bands. But it's one you should be aware of. Most bands will need some kind of backing if not a deal in place to get there. I have known of some unsigned bands who have been able to get onto the event but the cost to an average band is around a minimum of £2,000 (flights, accommodation, food, etc). The event has helped launch the careers of bands such as The White Stripes, The Killers, Norah Jones, James Blunt and helped The Arctic Monkeys blow up in the US. Media from around the world along with music industry personnel descend upon the town for the week-long event. A&R will be there in droves checking out the who is who of bands picked to play.

I would say this is a major event to get onto but even then, like everything else, just because you get the chance to play doesn't mean you will get a deal afterwards. Most bands who play there will have a buzz about them already with the media blowing things out of proportion as usual. You can make a good impression at SXSW and it's definitely worth a shot at getting onto the event. Just make sure if you apply you are ready and can get yourselves over there.

# FOR THOSE ABOUT TO ROCK ...

And here we are at the end of the book. Oh my god! It's a strange feeling reaching the end, but I hope I achieved what I set out to do, which was to help you understand the entire process of thinking for yourself and giving you an infrastructure to implement in the creating of your own careers. There will be more from the Rock and Roll Times set up so keep an eye on **www.therockandrolltimes.co.uk,** and don't forget to drop by and say hi sometime. You have enough in this book to get moving and I wish you the best of luck in all you do. The future is yours to create and don't let anyone tell you otherwise. For those about to Rock, I salute you all!

Love and hugs

*Will*

# Reference Materials

The following websites were used in referencing of materials and articles during the making of this book. Each website is a goldmine of articles and interviews from music industry personnel that cover all the chapters in this book, from A&R, publishing, touring, merchandise, websites, agents, promoters, recording, management, legal advice, press, accounts, setting up a record label and many other things.

www.taxi.com

www.vocalist.org

www.wikipedia.com

www.bbc.co.uk/radio1/onemusic/industry

www.ifpi.org

www.masteringworld.com

www.a1cds.com

The only book I referenced from was the *Home Recording Handbook* published by **www.flametreepublishing.com** which is a great resource and I urge you to buy a copy.

# Index